Finding
Soul on the
Path of
Orișa

Finding Soul on the Path of Orisa

A WEST AFRICAN SPIRITUAL TRADITION

Tobe Melora Correal
Iyalorisha Omilade

THE CROSSING PRESS

The Crossing Press
www.crossingpress.com

A division of Ten Speed Press
P.O. Box 7123
Berkeley, California 94707
www.tenspeed.com

Cover design and illustration by Nathan Walker
Text design by Nathan Walker
Edited by Colleen Sell

Library of Congress Cataloging-in-Publication Data

Correal, Tobe Melora.
   Finding soul on the path of Orisa : a West African spiritual
   tradition / by Tobe Melora Correal.
      p. cm.
   Includes bibliographical references.
   ISBN 1-58091-149-8 (pbk.)
   1. Yoruba (African people)—Religion. 2. Orishas. I. Title.

BL2480.Y6 C665 2002
299'.68333—dc21   2001042253

First printing, 2002
Printed in the United States

1 2 3 4 5 6 7 8 9 10—07 06 05 04 03

Dedication

For Sunshine Akanella, for being willing to get well
and for making this book possible.
And for my amazing and delightful nieces,
Zoe, Amara, and Nia Bleu:
May life give them everything they need
To grow into self-actualized, self-loving,
brave-hearted women.

Table of Contents

Acknowledgments

Sadly, I have far less room than I need to publicly thank all the individuals who have supported this book in some way. That said, I am deeply grateful to:

My precious mom, Vega Melissa Correal, Obatala's daughter. Her support for this book and encouragement of my many creative passions have been unshakable. *Adupe,* mama.

My ancestors and the Orisa, who bring me healing and beauty beyond measure, for so patiently teaching me about the true nature of their love.

My Godmother, Gladys "Bobi" Cespedes-Obalade, santera and spiritualist extraordinaire, who lined my spiritual pockets with plush velvet, then filled them with diamonds and gold. I could ask for no better foundation than the one she gave me.

My Godfather Cyril "Skip" Butler-Omitolokun, for his tender loving care and for being such a shining example of Yemaya's strength and goodness.

Yvette Cortez-Eyeleti, my former wife and partner, who was at my side almost from the beginning of this project. Through numerous rejection letters, the tedious and frustrating hunt for a publisher, endless rewrites, and last minute crises, she supported, sustained, and loved me. I could not have done this without you. *Gracias pa' todo.*

My editor at Crossing Press, Colleen Sell, for caring for my book as if it were her own; Brie Mazurek, my editor at Ten Speed Press, for having such a clear ear; Silver Tyler, formerly of the Ann Rittenberg Literary Agency, for seeing the jewel beneath the very rough edges of this project's early stages; and the Serpent Source Foundation for Women Artists, for awarding me a generous grant at a critical time in my writing.

My peeps, Amara, Frances, Birrell, Donna, Liz, and Bishop; and asha bandele, Tara Hunter, Nancy Brady Cunningham, Sim-El Fatunmishe, and Richelle, for facilitating connections.

Aya de Leon, who holds the vision of what's coming when I am unable to, for witnessing me with so much love, and for nonstop encouragement and excellent ideas.

My therapist, Catherine Tahmin, a woman of exceptional heart and wisdom, for being a channel for Orisa's renewal, and for giving me such a strong and compassionate container in which to grieve, rage, and heal.

Saidiya Hartman, an amazing writer and dearest friend, for being at my side when I took my first terrified steps toward writing this book. Her tender care kept me afloat during rough waters. Time and again, she insisted I had the right to write and reminded me that though the road is long it is never futile.

The fantastic and honey-licious Gina Gold, for helping me get through what felt like an endless abyss of dreary days, for feeding me daily doses of encouragement along with her ferocious and brilliant humor, for making sure I stay honest, for loving me even when I mess up, and for mad fun in New York City. Bow down!

Prologue

The Yoruba religion is the science of allowing God to flow through you, so that each breath becomes a prayer, and as God breathes, you breathe.

—John Mason

I was in my early twenties when I first discovered these words. In those early years of my spiritual development, they were like gold for me. With a simple, clarifying grace, they spoke to my deepest yearning for a life of reverence and bore the promise of blessings I knew the tradition held.

Yet, I was full of questions. *How do I let God flow through me? What if I don't like the feel of God's breath in me? If I'm angry or sad, are those breaths still prayers, still God*? Though Mason's words resonated with me, I had no idea how to apply his teachings to my daily life. I had found a spiritual path that beckoned me, but I had no map or compass to guide my journey.

My first spiritual guidance came from my mother. Though she never took my brother and me to church or espoused a particular religion or spiritual doctrine, she taught us that God lives in all things, especially in nature. One of my sweetest childhood memories is of my mom pointing out the wonder of a blossoming tree as we walked together one spring afternoon and saying to the tree, "Look how special you are! Thank you for being so beautiful."

My mother's hunger for spiritual knowledge and her constant struggle to find and stay connected with an accessible, generous Divine Presence were a prevailing influence throughout my childhood. She studied metaphysics and the Tarot, her favorite being the Death card, which says death paves the way for new life. One of her favorite deities was the Hindu goddess Kali, who transforms via annihilation. Her fascination with rebirth through death would later deeply affect my own spiritual work.

When we were growing up, mama also kept altars, which were made of simple, carefully selected and placed representations of Divinity: shells, candles, rocks found in sacred places, a special swatch of cloth, a prayer handwritten on pretty paper. My mom's reverence for the natural world and for creativity had a profound and lasting impact on how I would worship as an adult.

Although my mother's emotional anguish often distracted her from her children's needs, she encouraged my intuitive nature in small but significant ways. When I told her I'd seen a man standing in the air, she acknowledged I'd seen a spirit and asked me to describe him. When I confided my fear of a group of bullies at the bus stop, she taught me how to make myself invisible and how to move danger away from me. She told me that intention was the essence of magic. She also admonished me to do to others only what I would want to come back to me—because come back it would, three times over. Shortly after my graduation from high school, my mom took me to a ritual led by one of her coworkers, a voluptuous and kindhearted Wiccan priestess. That small gathering honoring the ancestors sparked the beginning of my conscious intention to pursue an Earth-centered spiritual life. But my mother's Wicca friend soon moved to Great Britain, and I didn't know how to find the spiritual guidance I craved. So I continued to feel called to a spiritual life and yet adrift at the same time.

Then I began taking African dance. Near the studio was a botanica, a store for practitioners of Orisa tradition, then most widely known in the United States as Santeria. One afternoon on my way home from class, I stopped in to browse. A feeling of familiarity, of home, filled me. The books and artifacts spoke of God in nature, of spirits and ritual, of altars and magic. From that day forward, I read everything I could find about Orisa and soon discovered John Mason.

Mason wrote of prayer in a very different way from the other books on Orisa I was reading. His concept went beyond praying only in ceremony and in front of shrines. It extended further than petitioning the deities for assistance and giving thanks to the ancestors. It was prayer as a quality of awareness and a state of being. In Mason's view, the world is a sacred landscape, and a seamless connection exists between God and all things in Creation—between God and me. This was a spiritual path I could envision myself walking along. It was prayer I could taste on my tongue.

I immersed myself in literature about Yoruba tradition and soon realized I needed to study with an elder. But I had moved to a small beach town where none were available to me. So, I continued trying to apply what I was learning from books to my daily life. I confided my fears and dreams to *Yemaya*, goddess of salt waters, cycles, and tides. In my journal, I wrote little prayer-poems to Elegua, opener of doors. I created altars like the ones with which I'd grown up, but with the Orisa or the ancestors in mind. Like my mother, I collected rocks, shells, and other altarpieces from nature and placed them next to candles and prayers to the deities, which I wrote on brightly colored paper.

Also like my mother, I lived with a gray cloud of depression hovering over me. My soul was in need of healing, and I began taking my struggles and pain to the Orisa. I'd walk the seashores and mountaintops surrounding my home, praying simply and timidly. I'd think to myself: *Surely, I am insignificant to these great deities. How dare I call upon Yemaya, Mother of the World, and Elegua, the Creator's right hand, without full knowledge of and formal commitment to Yoruba tradition? Why should they pay attention to me when I don't even know the proper rituals and the right prayers?*

But despite my lack of knowledge, guidance, and experience, the Orisa were clearly listening. However improper my sacrifice to Yemaya, Mother of the Oceans, I could feel her healing waters lapping against and smoothing the hardened places within me. However inadequate my prayers were to Elegua, Keeper of the Threshold and Guardian of Life-Force Energy, he nonetheless responded to them.

I always knew my solitary learning was in preparation for finding an elder to guide me deep into this powerful tradition. I now believe that the most viable road to Orisa is one charted by those who know the full depth, breadth, and power of the tradition. The best guides are Yoruba elders, who've had extensive experience with Orisa's rituals and practices and seen lives, particularly their own, transformed by them. Had the right teacher been available to me sooner, I would have jumped at the chance. Still, I learned some valuable lessons during the solo leg of my journey—the most important being that the strength and quality of my spiritual path were ultimately up to me. Even the most highly evolved teachers can't protect me from myself or do my work for me.

After a few years of searching alone for the soul of the tradition, I was ready to commit formally to the Orisa and to ask their help in healing myself. I returned to the San Francisco Bay Area in search of an elder with whom to study. Soon, I found my godmother, an Afro-Cuban priestess, and began an intense ten-year period of religious schooling. She taught a simple, down-to-earth approach to the tradition: Ancestors first. Learn the rituals, but don't get caught up in formality. Talk to the Orisa anywhere, any time, about anything, and they will hear you. Don't let priestly status or adornments blind you; that which is most Divine is usually invisible to the human eye. When in ritual, make your every thought and word a prayer, and be conscious of what you are praying for. Make altars for the gods, but love Orisa with what you have—it is always enough.

Yet, for all my sincere desire, good intentions, and earnest attempts, Mason's way of praying remained out of my reach. My godmother and I eventually separated, with much heartbreak on both our parts. I added her spiritual gifts to those my mother had given me and began to examine the aspects of traditional Orisa practice that did not fit my own spirituality.

I saw how some people misused the tradition in order to live on the surface of their lives. I realized even faithful initiates could miss out on the core values of our tradition. I found that many folks incorporated entirely too much fear into their practice of the tradition—fear of the gods, black magic, vengeful ancestors, and the unknown. Others used sacrifice as a bargaining tool—"If I give you this, will you give me that?" Some used ritual as a way of avoiding responsibility—"I know I've made a mess of things, but in exchange for this offering, will you clean it up for me?" I became aware of great pain within myself and others, pain that sometimes was transformed into bitter feuds fueled by malicious gossip, power struggles, and egos run amok. I also noticed blind spots in my own practice, places within myself and in my relationships where I was not paying attention.

As time went on, I grew convinced that inner work must accompany religious practice. While paying homage to the ancestors, we must also face our personal demons and reckon with the havoc they wreak on our lives. While honoring the deities, we must also learn to love ourselves and treat each other with greater kindness. Otherwise, our religion becomes a desolate field, littered with false faces and unfinished business. And our practice becomes a mere flicker of the transforming brilliance our ancestors intended it to be.

For a while in my efforts to breathe with God, I donned a mask of spiritual correctness, saying all the right prayers and performing my ceremonial tasks perfectly. Behind closed doors, I was a mess—depressed, self-hating, out of touch with Divinity and myself. I'd made the mistake of assuming I could find God's breath by taking the tools of the tradition and applying them to the obstacles in my outer life. But the real barriers were within me, and they were blocking my ability to embody Mason's teachings.

In time and with hard work, I realized that in order for God to flow steadily through me, I had to discover and show my true face and embrace the things I feared and despised. I had to look at things about my life and the people in it, past and present, that I didn't really want to know or deal with. I was forced into the awkward but essential process of unmasking and revealing a more authentic me. I had to own up to my inability to see God in others and in myself. And in this way I began the much harder work of learning to channel the flow of God in genuine, tangible ways.

That work continues, and so far there is no end in sight. I still curse too much and gossip too much. I too often approach difficult issues sideways rather than head on, and I show too little compassion for others and myself. I still flash my nasty underside to those closest to me, and they and others in my life can speak to ways in which I've been care-less and dishonest with them. Still, Mason's words and the questions they posed for me continue to guide my spiritual life. I live intimately with them, so that I might absorb them into my heart and embody them every day. And in learning about Orisa tradition, I continue to learn about God, humanity, and myself.

Over the years, I have slightly reframed Mason's original thought. I now understand Orisa practice to be less science and more art. I see it less as spiritual mastery and more as a commitment to marshal all my inner resources in doing this spiritual work day by day.

I have been walking the path of Orisa for most of my adult life. This book is a reflection of that still-unfolding journey. I hope you will find it helpful in navigating your own way along the path and deep into the soul of Orisa.

Introduction

Orisa (pronounced *Or-ee'-shah*) is a branch of the indigenous, Earth-centered religion of the Yoruba people of southwestern Nigeria. It has existed for at least four thousand years; some anthropologists believe it has been practiced for as many as eight thousand years. The tradition spread from Africa primarily to Cuba and Brazil via the trans-Atlantic slave route of the nineteenth century. Cuban immigrants to New York City brought the religion to the United States in the 1930s and '40s. Today, as many as 75 million people worldwide practice some version of the tradition: Yoruba or Orisa (Nigeria and the United States), Santeria (Cuban, syncretized with Catholicism), Yoruba-Lukumi (Afro-Cuban, non-syncretized), Candomble (Brazil), Shango Baptist (Trinidad), and the Ifa priesthood (Nigeria and the Americas).

The Yoruba faith is a monotheistic tradition that recognizes one God who speaks and works on Earth through a pantheon of gods and goddesses called *Orisa*. The ancestors, or *egun*, assist and support the living in their daily lives. The tradition's deepest mysteries and teachings are contained in a body of oral scriptures, called *odu*, which have passed from elders to devotees for countless generations. These are some of the basic concepts and components that form the foundation of all Yoruba-based traditions.

Yoruba religion is a way of life. It is the spiritual practice of working in loving relationship not only with the deities but also with the ancestors. It is seeking to know the sacred nature of life—the breath of God flowing through all things. It is the holistic integration of all aspects of our being—bodies, feelings, thoughts, and energies—in order to restore wholeness where there is fragmentation and balance where there is disarray.

For all its power and beauty, Orisa, like most traditions that fall outside dominant Western religions, has been much maligned and feared. Despite the tradition's growing acceptance around the globe, many misconceptions about its principles and practices remain. With this book, I hope to remove some of the misinformation and prejudice surrounding this richly layered, soul-enhancing spiritual path. Though I was schooled and initiated in the Yoruba-Lukumi branch of the tradition, the basic ideas presented in these pages are relevant to a broad range of Orisa practitioners, regardless of their religious roots. To be as inclusive as possible, I've cited English, Spanish, and Yoruba terms throughout the book. When referring to the tradition and its practitioners, I use Yoruba and Orisa interchangeably. Though differences exist between the various branches of this lushly canopied spiritual tree, the fundamental teachings set forth by our ancient Yoruba elders form the backbone of all variations of the religion. All branches of Yoruba-based religions share certain things, some positive, others negative. One of the more damaging of these commonalities is fear.

Fear—among both those inside the tradition and those outside it—plays a dominant and often toxic role in the Yoruba legacy. Among practitioners, fear becomes a veil that obscures the full wonder of the tradition. Among outsiders, fear and its cousin ignorance stem primarily from inaccurate, often fictitious depictions of African religions in the news and entertainment media. Abuses of power among Yoruba practitioners add fuel to the fires of fear and intolerance. To the uninformed, the mere mention of Orisa worship is likely to conjure up images of practitioners hacking off chicken heads in wanton sacrificial rituals; of wild-eyed witch doctors casting evil curses on innocent people; of possessed initiates gesticulating and chanting incoherently; of animism, black magic, and what is disparagingly referred to as voodoo.

The term *voodoo* is often slapped on any ritual from Africa that the Western mind doesn't understand. The religious system known as voodoo originated in Haiti but has its roots in Dahomey, West Africa. The word *voodoo* is derived from the Fon word *vodun,* which means spirit or deity. The Fon people and the Yoruba are neighbors and share many ideas about life, nature, and spirituality. Both the Fon and Yoruba respect the power of words, drums, leaves, and ritual, and a few of their gods even have similar names. Nevertheless, Fon and Yoruba are two distinct traditions, each with its own practices and teachings, only some of which intersect.

Another common misconception is that all African spiritual traditions are synonymous with black magic, meaning magic that is worked for evil ends. Black magic is part of the tradition, but only a small percentage of devotees use it. These wayward priests and priestesses are no different from their counterparts in any other religion, who misuse sacred energies to frighten, exploit, and harm others.

There are also myriad misconceptions surrounding any spiritual practice that involves possession and animal sacrifice. Most African traditions, including Yoruba-based ones, do work with trance and blood sacrifice, that is, the ritualistic killing of animals (never humans). In fact, virtually every world religion has or has had similar practices, and such rituals are always rooted in the desire to pay reverence. Although it is taboo for any devotee (except between initiates) to disclose how any of our rituals are performed, I can tell you that in Yoruba practices, as in many religions, blood symbolizes life. By offering blood to the Orisa, we enliven our relationship with the gods, stimulating and fortifying our spiritual unity with them.

In Cuba, cycles of religious persecution periodically forced slaves who were devotees to practice the tradition underground. They disguised their African gods as Catholic saints, a process called *syncretization*, in order to ensure the survival of rituals which their owners would otherwise have forbidden. Although the strategy worked and the rituals survived slavery, syncretization left a residue of fear and an air of secrecy in its wake.

In the United States, the tradition's survival and our ability to practice it freely no longer depend on subterfuge and going underground. Nonethless, many practitioners stubbornly hold to the contention that we must keep our tradition private. This self-enforced invisibility prevents non-practitioners from seeing Orisa practitioners for who we really are—their neighbors, coworkers, and friends. And it makes it more difficult to dispel misconceptions about our tradition.

Infighting among different branches, communities, godparents, and practitioners is another destructive force within the tradition. Though Yoruba initiates come in every stripe, intolerance exists among us. Some branches consider themselves the true keepers of the tradition and look down on other groups whose practices are often more similar than different from theirs. Certain communities downplay the tradition's "primitive" African origins, while others criticize those practicing a "slave master's" version of the religion.

Then there are the folks who want to keep out white people, gays, lesbians, and anyone else they consider to be "other." However, in the eyes of God, as the ancient elders and as Mason described it, where we come from, what we look like, and our sexual orientation have no bearing on our right to embrace Orisa's teachings. It is our responsibility to work through these issues so that we are able to see the breath of God in everything and everyone. Orisa does not belong to any particular person or group. Yoruba initiates come from every part of the globe, and as our numbers swell, our diversity increases. So too must our tolerance, understanding, and inclusion of one another.

Though some devotees choose religious communities that are relatively homogeneous, others choose communities where differences are embraced and cooperation flourishes. There are many Orisa *houses* that welcome people of varied backgrounds and that focus their united energies toward the greater good of one another, their communities, and the world. In many of our communities, the diverse family of Orisa works together toward a common goal—that of celebrating and preserving the teachings that our ancestors left in our care.

Such flexibility has been one of Orisa's hallmarks, an enduring attribute that has allowed our tradition to survive and thrive for many centuries. Consequently, I witnessed events in sacred spaces in Nigeria that would disturb my elders in the United States. And some of our common perspectives in America made no sense to priests I met in Africa. While Brazilian practitioners remain novices for seven years or more, the novice period lasts a year and seven days in the United States and sometimes less in Cuba. Such differences do not exist because one group is more authentic, more informed, or more entitled to the teachings than another. Yoruba tradition, as it was intended and as many practice it, accepts variation in culture, geography, language, circumstance, and human individuality. Indeed, Yoruba tradition stresses the importance of staying open and of respecting differences. These tenets have enabled Orisa elders to pass on these ancient teachings from one diaspora to another, adapting them as needed, yet retaining their sacred essence.

Somewhere along the way, however, I believe we lost an essential piece of that essence. That is why I have written a book that focuses less on the outward manifestations of our practices and more on the inner life of practitioners. While staying close to my tradition's flexible roots, I present a more introspective approach based on my belief that a person's spiritual development is synonymous with inner work. I have titled this book *Finding Soul on the Path of Orisa*, and the word "finding" is important and intentional. It implies that the soul, our deep spiritual center, is always present. We need only turn inward to draw on its power during our journey of struggle and transformation.

In homage to the deity Elegua, Owner of the Cross-roads—whose magic number is three and with whom we Yorubas begin all our sacred work—the book is divided into three sections. Part one looks at some of the basic teachings that form the metaphysical underpinnings of the tradition and at how we might apply those teachings to our daily lives. Part two deals with the ancestors and provides a guide to building authentic and meaningful relationships with the spirits. Part three gives an overview of the tradition's structure and covers the purpose and function of the rites of initiation.

Embracing Orisa teachings as the ancestors intended them requires multi-layered work: studying ritual, divine laws, and principles; looking deep within and learning about ourselves; living with authenticity and passion; and honoring Divinity in its varied forms. Perhaps more than anything, it means becoming conscious in our relationships with God, the ancestors, one another, and ourselves. In so doing, as we walk the Orisa path we will find the nourishment for what Mason so wisely saw as our central spiritual task—the practice of breathing with God in each moment.

PART ONE

A YORUBA VISION OF LIFE AND GOD

Several thousand years ago in the lush tropics of West Africa, a group of elders among the Yoruba-speaking people of Nigeria channeled divine teachings while in trance. In a state of deep meditation, the elders spoke in the voices of revered ancestors, the ancient ones who had lived before them, the *egun*. The ancestral voices told of a Supreme Being and the miracle of Creation. They spoke of the nature and purpose of all things in the universe and of the divine energy—the breath of God—flowing between the heavens and Earth. The elders shared their sacred gifts of *ogbon* (wisdom), *imo* (knowledge), and *oye* (understanding) with their people, creating a rich body of ritual and oracular scriptures, the *odu*. For generations, Yoruba elders have taught their people how to live in harmony with nature and each other and close to God.

How do these ancient teachings support what Mason describes as the central purpose of human existence: to develop awareness of the sacred essence flowing in all things? What information did those long-ago elders leave behind, encoded in the beliefs and laws of their spiritual tradition, to support our efforts to achieve a heightened consciousness—to breathe with God? To answer these questions, we must begin at the beginning, with the Yoruba concepts of divinity and creation. These teachings comprise a vast body of information that is best learned at the knees of your elders, the Orisa priests and priestesses who serve as your guides. This and other books about the Yoruba tradition can also help you.

The concepts presented here are by no means inclusive. They are merely the ones that I, as a student of this tradition making my own journey toward deeper understanding, feel are some of the most important. They are also among the fundamental metaphysical ideas that inform the core practices and daily experiences of practitioners around the world.

In the Yoruba cosmos, there is one Supreme Being— the Source, the Almighty Owner of the entire universe, God—whose work on this galaxy is carried out by one Creator, whose work on Earth is aided by 401 gods and goddesses. Both Source (Olorun) and Creator (Olodumare) exist in the Invisible Realm (Ikole Orun), while the "helper" gods (the Orisa) exist as divine immortals on Earth (Ikole Aye). The energies of Source flow into and join with the energies of the Creator, which combined flow through and join with the manifold energies of the Orisa, which then flow through all that exists in Creation.

Chapter I

In the Beginning

Yoruba divinity actually begins *before* the beginning, with Olorun, the Supreme Being and Source of the entire universe. According to Yoruba teachings, Olorun is so profound an intelligence and mystery, such an intense force, that we can never fully understand what It is or how It organizes and runs the universe. Although often referred to by practitioners as Father and He, Olorun is neither male nor female.[1] For the sake of simplicity and also because it feels comfortable for me personally, I often use the feminine pronoun when referring to Olorun. In truth, Olorun is an infinitely divine force that is minimized by assigning it either gender. Indeed, Olorun's composition and potency are beyond the capacity of the human mind to comprehend, let alone define, and beyond the capacity of the human body to experience consciously with our physical senses.

Although the Supreme Being is beyond our intellectual and physical grasp, Yoruba teachings maintain that a fundamental oneness exists between God and Creation. For Yoruba practitioners, holiness resides within all things of nature, both animate and inanimate. People who look at life through an *either/or* lens may have trouble with the concept of every single thing being at one with an indefinable entity that we cannot touch, see, hear, smell, taste, or fully explain. How, they might ask, can something so elusive be at the same time so integral to who and what we are? If we can never physically experience or even describe Olorun, how can we find oneness with God here on Earth? How can we human beings live spiritually connected to the Supreme Being? How can we breathe God's breath in every moment?

The Yoruba path follows a *both/and* approach to living,[2] which allows for and embraces all facets of any situation, even forces that appear to cancel out each other. This ability to see multiple sides of things makes it possible for us to accept the idea that God is both near us and far away. It enables us to acknowledge that although God is more powerful than we can envision or articulate, God is in our breath, our blood, and every moment of our daily lives.

Creation

How did Olorun, the Owner and Source of all that is, create Earth and its inhabitants? And how do we fit into this creation? This little story helps to explain this divine mystery:

> *Way up in Ikole Orun, beyond the place where suns are born, there is a gigantic water pot, owned by the Supreme God, Olorun. Although no one has ever seen Olorun's pot, it is known far and wide as the biggest, most beautiful, and strongest of all water pots—overflowing with the purest, sweetest, and most sparkling water. The elders tell ancient stories that hail the magnificence of Olorun's pot,*

which the old ones refer to as the Beginning of All Things. So powerful is the pot's magic that it creates entire worlds. And even though divine water pours constantly from this ever-overflowing pot, it never ceases to flow and always remains full.

One day Olorun decided She wanted to begin creating physical matter in the universe. She had attempted this several times before by flooding the heavens with the magic waters of Her great pot, but each time She encountered the same dilemma. Because the water contained so much of Her greatness and power, it was too hot and scorched the universe before anything had a chance to develop.

And Olorun was pressed for time, since as the Supreme Being, She was busy maintaining order in the cosmos. So, to facilitate Her work creating the universe, Olorun decided She needed to find an assistant and a way to cool down the pot's scalding waters.

After some thought, Olorun came upon a way to resolve the situation. She remembered that countless eons ago She had made another water pot, one slightly smaller than Hers, but still enormous and magical. She had given it to her oldest child, Olodumare, who placed it in the heavens a little below Olorun's palace and watched over it. Olorun sent for Olodumare to visit Her so they could discuss Her plan, which would be supervised by Olorun and carried out by Olodumare. This was the plan: As Olorun's magic water flowed over the wide rim and down the great belly of Her pot, Olodumare would hold Her own pot at just the right angle to catch the water as it fell from the upper heavens. Next, Olodumare would mix into Olorun's water some of Her own power and beauty along with a little bit of Her blessed saliva to cool the water to just the right temperature for creating matter in the universe. Olodumare would then pour their combined and cooled juices into the lower heavens, thereby creating the stars, life forms, and all matter and energy in the universe. That was the first part of Olorun's request.

Olorun had another task for her daughter: She asked Her to look after one particular spot in the cosmos, where Olorun wanted to create several planets, including a small one She would call Earth. Olorun asked Olodumare to create and take care of Earth. She was to make sure it had everything it needed to evolve and develop over time, and to put the proper rhythms and cycles into place. Olorun suggested that Olodumare share the work with Her children, the Orisa. She said:

> After my waters have cooled a bit in your great vessel, give your children a drink from the pot. Then send them down to Earth to pour my waters—each one in his or her own way—into everything that you will create there on my behalf but in your name. Although I ask that you check with me every now and then, I trust you will put the very best of your goodness into this work. I am too busy and needed in too many places to worry about all the details, so I'll leave those up to you. Also my hands, unlike

yours, are too old and hot to cool my waters. Although I am and will always remain the Most Powerful, First, and Oldest, you will be my second in command, known and revered as the Creator, an infinitely great and powerful force.

When Olorun finished speaking, Olodumare, filled with emotion and gratitude, fell to Her knees. She thanked Her mother for giving Her such an important task and promised to put Her whole heart and complete attention into doing Her job. Brimming with joy, She left Olorun's palace and immediately set about the blessed work Her mother had assigned Her.

To this day, Olodumare remains in the lower heavens, fulfilling Her promise to Olorun, creating and taking care of life on Earth as well as the planets and stars surrounding it. Her children, the Orisa, still drink Olorun's magic waters and still pour that magic into everything on Earth. Olorun, Owner and Source of all things, continues to direct and oversee it all from Her great palace atop the highest peak in Ikole Orun.[3]

Although Olorun is the Source of Creation, Olodumare directs the actual shaping of existence. In his book *Olodumare: God in Yoruba Belief*, Bolaji Idowu lists several of Olodumare's many praise names: the Great Enabler, Author of All Things and Events, the One Whose Being Spreads Over the Whole Extent of the Earth, and the One Whose Works Are Done to Perfection. For the Yoruba, Olodumare functions as the creative divine intelligence, birthing and sustaining all matter. She does so without error and allows only that which has met Her approval to manifest.

Olodumare, like Olorun, is often designated as male, but like Olorun, Olodumare also transcends gender. The tendency to refer to Olodumare and Olorun as male is the product of patriarchal thinking and cultural systems. Because Olodumare represents the sacred womb of Creation—and because women create new life through their wombs—I chose to use the feminine pronoun for this story. Nonetheless, please remember that although feminizing the Creator is, in a basic sense, appropriate to this story, it is not metaphysically accurate. While Olodumare and Olorun encompass both feminine and masculine energies, neither is exclusively male or female.[4]

While it is entirely appropriate to refer to Olorun, Olodumare, and Orisa as God, Yoruba teachings are very clear that there is only one Source, Olorun. Olodumare and Orisa perform functions as extensions of Olorun's unchanging Essence. Their divine powers derive from Olorun; without Her they could not even exist.

Orisa

Although the Orisa are the youngest players in Yoruba cosmogony, they are vitally important to the lives of Yoruba practitioners. We praise Orisa, not because we are animistic, polytheistic, or fetishistic. We are not confused about Orisa's role in Creation. Yoruba is a monotheistic tradition. We do not believe in multiple Gods with a capital G; to us Orisa are gods, subordinate to the Supreme One. We know the difference between Source (Olorun) and Creator (Olodumare), and between Creator and Her messengers (Orisa).

We also know it is the Orisa who give us a mechanism for the great Force that created the universe. We know it is these children of Olodumare who make Source's energy, Olorun's waters, accessible to our human experience. We love and worship Orisa, because, though they are not God as Source or God as Creator, they are God revealing divinity to us in tangible ways that we, within the limits of our human capacities, can understand.

Yoruba practitioners know that God "manifests Itself to humans in a multiplicity of forms"[5] and that Orisa energies are living embodiments of this multiplicity. We understand that, at Olorun's request, Olodumare assigned guardianship of specific life processes and activities to each Orisa. At the same time, She gave them particular areas of expertise and influence for helping humanity and all life on Earth to evolve. Every Orisa expresses itself in a unique way—through certain environments, substances, colors, plants, creatures, actions, anatomical parts, personalities, forces of nature, circumstances, conditions, rhythms, and tones. Each Orisa has specific things to teach and unique qualities to give us. (If you are unfamiliar with the qualities and attributes of the deities, there are books available that can provide this information. Several are listed in the reference section at the back of this book.)

The Orisa share with the world the specific "divine ray"[6] of Olodumare's force with which they have been enlivened. Orisa are divinity and they do possess the powers of the sacred, but only to the extent that Olodumare allows and only within the parameters given to Olodumare by Olorun. Under the direction of the Supreme Being, the Creator determines the Orisa's responsibilities, and the Orisa carry out their duties according to God's will.

Although the Orisa significantly impact human affairs and our world, their existence is not contingent upon ours. In fact, some of the oldest Orisa were given their assignments long before the beginnings of life on Earth. Should human beings one day cease to exist, Olodumare's work on Earth will continue to unfold, supported by the activities and energies of Orisa.

It is precisely because Yoruba tradition recognizes the singular greatness of Olorun that the Orisa are so important to practitioners. We acknowledge ourselves as the children of Orisa, who are the children of the Creator, who is the child of Source, the Supreme Being. We understand that all that pouring of divine water—from Olorun to Olodumare, through the Orisa, and into Creation—has endowed all life with the sacredness of the One Source. We realize that the Orisa are immediately responsible for filling our world and each of us with Olorun's magic.

Because we know this about the Orisa, we revere them and we thank them. We pay special attention to them through our rituals and shrines, in private and in community, because our relationship with Orisa keeps us mindful of the power, beauty, and presence of Olodumare. In loving Orisa, we acknowledge the flow of Olorun's essence running through our lives. For the Yoruba, the more intimately we know Orisa, the more intimately we know God.

---

1. Babalawo Fagbemi Fasina, oral instruction.

2. Ibid.

3. Although the story is mine, Babalawo Fagbemi Fasina explained to me the concepts and principles expressed here.

4. Babalawo Fagbemi Fasina, oral instruction.

5. Fa'lokun Fatunmbi, *Iba'se Orisa.*

6. Iyalorisha Obalade, oral instruction.

Chapter Two

Living Intimately with Orisa

Fa'lokun Fatunmbi has written that one of the fundamental concerns of Yoruba tradition "is the ongoing process of gaining deeper insight into the mysteries (or 'children') of Olodumare that have a direct impact on human life."[7] The mysteries to which he refers are the Orisa. As important as this insight is, it is just a starting point on the journey to understanding and ultimately to living the Yoruba way. To embrace this path fully, we must work not only to understand Orisa, but also to deepen our relationships with them. Increasing our intimacy with Orisa further informs and inspires our insights. Just as knowledge *of* Orisa enhances our closeness *with* Orisa, so too does amplifying how we *experience* Orisa deepen what we *know* about them.

It is not enough to become skilled in the outer mechanics of the tradition—to simply learn the oral histories and merely perform the traditional songs, prayers, rituals, ceremonies, customs, and divinations. None of these alone will automatically unveil the most resonant and meaningful gifts of Orisa. The number of years we've accumulated in initiation, praying elaborately in the Yoruba tongue, and speaking knowledgeably about divine concepts are only relevant to the degree that they help us establish and maintain intimate relationship with Orisa. Only then do these practices allow us to uncover the deep, soulful nature of the tradition.

The most essential ingredient in our soul's nourishment is the steady cultivation of a holistic connectedness with Orisa that touches every part of us—physical, emotional, intellectual, psychological, and spiritual. Nurturing this closeness requires that we open all facets of our lives to the Orisa's teachings and allow their energies to transform us. It entails learning to recognize the ways in which the deities show themselves in our relationships, our bodies, our communities, and nature. It means being willing to apprentice both our thinking and feeling selves to Orisa's mysteries, to being, as Alan Jones writes, "believer[s] with both passion and intelligence."[8]

So profound and vast are the mysteries held by Orisa that discovering, comprehending, and embracing them requires a journey of a lifetime. This journey will transform your view of yourself and the world. It will teach you about the physical and metaphysical. It will connect you to blessings from the past, while anchoring you in the present and ushering in your future. As with any journey, you will need directions, preparations, counsel, and assistance. These you must solicit and receive from your elders, those wise keepers of the tradition, who have preserved and passed along the rituals and teachings that the *egun* first whispered into their ears so many centuries ago. Though Yoruba elders and scholars have documented some of these teachings, there is far more to know than what has been written. What is more, you will encounter considerable variation in perspectives and approaches. That is fine and well. Our tradition allows, indeed encourages, practitioners to find their individual, authentic relationships with God.

You will find further guidance and support from the members of your chosen religious community, your Orisa "house" or *ile*. Since most godparents head a house, most followers become part of that community at least initially. Worshipping, celebrating, and sharing with others who also seek deep relationship with Orisa will help you understand and embody the Orisa way. Yet, no matter how much information and inspiration you receive from your community and elders, they do not have all the answers. They cannot carry you on your journey. They cannot give you intimacy with God. They cannot unlock your soul, so that Orisa can flow through you. Only you hold that key. And the only way to find it is to dig deep within, to see yourself as you really are, and to show yourself to Orisa.

Even when you follow this path within the encircling arms of community, you will walk much of the way alone, seeking and absorbing the varied energies of Orisa through private prayer, meditation, sacrifice, ritual, divination, self-reflection, and contemplation. In time, you will become aware of the constant presence of the Orisa, who, in reality, have accompanied you all along.

The first step in your journey is making the commitment, to yourself and God, to learn and live the Orisa way.

You must then back up that commitment with sincere intention and concerted action every step of the way. This is, believe me, easier said than done, but the fruits of your efforts will come.

If you answer the call to become soulfully connected to Orisa, if you strive to understand and get close to the deities, you will undoubtedly find yourself stretched and broadened by your spiritual practice. That is a good thing. The best spiritual life is challenging. It takes you away from what is safe and easy, and if you are fully engaged, through discomfort and unease.

Walking this path involves arduous, continuous work, some of which is bound to hurt, perplex, and frustrate you. It will expose what you most defend in yourself, but this exposure will deepen and liberate you. There are no alternate routes, no detours, to finding the soul on the path of Orisa. Only through devoting yourself to a spiritual practice that pushes you beyond your comfort zone can you get to the heart of these teachings. Only when you allow religion to be more than a book of rules or a means to get power can you internalize the fundamental truth about Creation: that our world overflows with the Sacred.

This truth is made so by the presence and flow of Olorun's waters and their potent magic, which in Yoruba tradition we call *ashe*.

Ashe

As Olorun's *ashe* pours from pot to pot into the bellies of Olodumare's children and then into our world and each of us, it leaves behind some of Olorun's magic at each juncture. This small but all-pervading portion of Olorun's essence saturates and makes holy all that it touches—and it touches everything.

Ashe is the divine essential nature of all things. It is the life force that radiates and streams from the Invisible Realm to the realm of matter, between the Orisa and us, and between all that exists in Creation. By filling the Orisa with Olorun's *ashe,* Olodumare utilizes them to bring us a message that says:

> *Wake up! Pay attention! Alive all around you and inside of you is the sacred energy of the Supreme Being and Me, the Creator. I, Olodumare, have channeled this divine source to my children, the Orisa, who flow It into everything on Earth as I create it. Open your eyes, and you will realize that nowhere is God absent—that no being, place, or thing, visible or invisible, living or inanimate, is without holiness. Look closely, and you will find something sacred everywhere and in everything. Witness with deep-seeing eyes, and you will see* ashe *revealed through the personalities of my children, the Orisa: in that rock where God is breathing, in that city where God is vibrating, in those waters where God is speaking, and in your soul where God is alive.*

Thus, the devotee who approaches the sea to pray or to make offerings is not simply praying before an ocean altar, as an uninformed observer might assume. Rather, they are addressing Yemaya—the particular *ashe,* or vital presence of God, embodied there. Knowing the sea has been bestowed with a specific "ray"[9] of the all-pervading Sacred Force, the Yoruba practitioner naturally acknowledges this radiance by addressing it directly.[10]

The Orisa's presence, their *ashe,* manifests itself on both tangible and intangible levels of existence. The manner and style with which each deity transmits its unique *ashe* to all things on Earth varies from one Orisa to the other, just as *ashe* expresses itself differently among people. Orisa may express their *ashe* with flamboyance (Shango), simplicity (Obatala), sensuality (Oshun), or generosity (Yemaya). I may express my *ashe* through clay or writing, you through performance or teaching, someone else through scientific research or singing, and another through cooking or gardening. *Ashe* comes in as many varieties as there are living things on Earth. And *ashe* may come quiet and loud, tender and abrupt, in bright colors and delicate hues, with soft curves and sharp edges.

These outer differences notwithstanding, the spark of Divinity, the magic water that the Orisa pour into everything, is essentially the same, regardless of the form it takes. Although each of Olodumare's creations—you and I, the waterfall and tree, the city and countryside—expresses *ashe* differently, *ashe* is *ashe*. Its sacred nature is fundamentally the same—equally blessed and equally present—wherever it is, regardless of the vessel holding it.

Even unwashed or unconsecrated items and beings have *ashe*. Yoruba consecration rituals acknowledge, draw out, amplify, and project *ashe,* aligning it with a particular energetic frequency, which is then directed toward a specific intention. People (and things) who have not undergone consecration rituals are not devoid of *ashe*; it is just that their *ashe* has not yet been ritually brought forth.

That Olodumare through Orisa has given Olorun's magic in equal measure to all things in Creation means that God's *ashe* is not conferred only upon a chosen few. Olodumare does not play favorites with Olorun's divine energy, giving more here and less there. Nor do some folks have *ashe* that is at its core better or more powerful than other people's. However, some people are exceptionally skilled or gifted in how they express their *ashe*. Even our wisest spiritual teachers and elders are given the same *ashe* as any other of Olodumare's creations. It's just that their intention and hard work have made their lives into clearer, more focused vessels, making the sacred in them more visible. Through meditation, prayer, self-reflection, and inner work, they have become more practiced and more consistent in expressing their indwelling *ashe* in ways that bring goodness to others and themselves. Because they see the mark of God on all things more clearly, they are more consistent in recognizing and honoring the ever-present magic of Olorun in our midst.

Whenever you encounter the notion that some people have better or more *ashe,* please consider the source of such claims. Often this idea is promoted for the sole purpose of gaining or maintaining power. The Creator does not concern Herself with quantifying or qualifying the sacredness of what She has created. Olodumare permeates every part of Creation with the same amount and same grade of the all-encompassing divine essence, *ashe.*

This principle holds true for everything Olodumare creates, including dwellers in the shadowlands, where war, poverty, addiction, hatred, sorcery, greed, and violence reign. As toxic as these realities are, the *ashe* in the perpetuators of evil is no less sacred than the *ashe* in Earth's most benevolent beings. Though evil persons may work against the greater good of the community and their own souls, they too are recipients of Olorun's *ashe,* vehicles for Olodumare's sacred activity, and vessels for Orisa energies.

That is not to say that Yoruba practitioners condone malevolent behavior and actions. It is always important and necessary to seek an end to oppression, violence, destruction, and injustice. At the same time, if we are to understand the essence of *ashe,* we must embrace this truth: All things are vessels of divine essence, intended to hold and pour forth *ashe,* even those found in the wide stretches of Creation where a great deal of suffering is inflicted and endured. We must accept the fact that the receptacles of *ashe* wear many faces, some of which are quite ugly in outward appearance, but whose *ashe* is no less sacred.

What distinguishes one thing from another—the priest and junkie, the architect and dancer, the war zone and temple, the mountain and sea—are not differences in the magic water they carry inside, but rather differences in the unique ways in which each embodies that magic in the outer world. While the personality cloaking each vessel varies from one to another, the basic nature of *ashe* in all things is exactly the same.[11]

In Yoruba theology, there is no devil, no heaven, and no hell. People do evil things on their own volition, not because evil is preordained or intrinsic to who they are. We each choose whether to use our *ashe* to help or harm others. *Ashe* itself is neither good nor bad. This concept is sometimes hard for us to understand. After all, we humans are quite skilled at using *ashe* for negative purposes. And nature's *ashe,* for all its goodness, can also behave badly. Some days, for example, the wind's *ashe* comes as a refreshing breeze to cool a sweltering afternoon. Other days it whips into a hurricane, ripping apart everything in its path. Regardless of how *ashe* is expressed in nature or how humans use it, *ashe* is a neutral energy. And all *ashe* is always holy.

Sacred Polarity

Yoruba teachings tell us that *ashe* expresses itself in two distinct and complimentary ways, in what Mason calls, "forces that build up and forces that tear down."[12] At any given moment in any given situation, the divine energy *(ashe)* that shapes and sustains Creation is moving between two fundamental poles—expanding and contracting, pushing out and pulling in, heating up and cooling down, being born and dying. In this context, death does not refer exclusively to the end of a physical life; it can also mean the death of any number of things: a belief, a behavior, a cycle, a relationship, a way of life.

In Yoruba tradition, life-enhancing and life-battering experiences both manifest something about God. Both are equally important elements of a single process: All things live and die so that they may be transformed and reborn, repeating the cycle again and again. The Yoruba understand that birth always accompanies death.

This universal principle—that for humans the life-force energy plays between two contrasting yet complimentary poles—exists, in one variation or another, in all spiritual philosophies. The Chinese call these forces *yin* and *yang*. But unlike yin and yang, which are assigned negative/positive, male/female, and active/passive attributes, the two sides of *ashe* are both active and without gender. The teachings also tell us that neither of these opposing energies is inherently positive or negative, and that both are necessary for life on Earth.

We find this same polarity in the ways each Orisa expresses the two contrasting sides of its unique *ashe*. Yemaya is the calm blue waters of the South Pacific and the raging tidal wave. Obatala is peace of mind and insanity. Elegua is an open door and a closed one. Oya is the queen of the cemetery who walks with the dead and also the breath of life circulating through our bodies. Each Orisa embodies a wide spectrum of attributes, spanning all variances of sweet and sour, gentle and rough, light and dark.

Once we understand these complex truths we can approach Olodumare's universe as a place where God reveals Itself through diverse spiritual energies. We learn that these energies are in constant flux, moving into balance and out of balance, fluctuating between various states of constructive and destructive activity. We embrace the knowledge that all aspects of Orisa are essential to the evolution of Creation and all are sacred.

The other more human side of that reality is that, even though Olodumare's *ashe* dwells in all things, many of us have lost the ability to see God in Its many expressions. Our minds and hearts have become clouded by *either/or* and *good/bad* perceptions. The ways of seeing that might allow us to experience the Holiness within us and around us have grown dull from lack of use. The spiritual muscles required for accessing the sacred essence at the core of all Olodumare's creations have atrophied. We have forgotten what is true about God, the universe, and ourselves.

Yoruba tradition gives us a spiritual means of cleaning our lenses and strengthening our muscles, so we can rise above limiting black-and-white thinking and see God through Orisa-illuminated eyes. Of course, we may not always like the part of God that Orisa is showing us. It may hurt; it may seem unjust; it may leave us feeling confused. But it is still God. Though we may not realize it and may frequently forget it, the fact remains: *God is all there is, there is nothing else, regardless of appearances.*[13] All *ashe*—whether it builds up or tears down—is God's *ashe*.

Take, for example, Oshun, the emanation of Olodumare's *ashe* that manifests in the fresh waters of the river. In her creative aspect, she is present wherever life-sweetening activity exists: springtime, new love, dancing in the streets at carnival, laughter. In her destructive role, she is the vulture stalking the dying, devouring decaying flesh, and picking the bones of the dead. Though we may take greater pleasure in Oshun's energy in its warm and inviting life-giving mode, Oshun in her guise as vulture is God working to keep balance in nature. In Yoruba tradition, we value all facets of Oshun's personality, because the buzzard's activity in the realm of death is as integral to life's processes as the birth of a child.

In this respect, "It is all God, and it is all good."[14] That doesn't mean it's all easy or fun, only that it's all sacred. Honoring the God-nature of people and things doesn't exempt us from suffering when that energy challenges us. When we recognize the neutral nature of *ashe* as well as the interdependence of the positive and negative elements of existence, we can discern the divine presence of life's brightness even among the shadows of our struggles.

When we embrace the dual essence of *ashe,* we stop running from the parts of Orisa we don't particularly enjoy, the stuff that tests us or brings us pain. We stop trying to control life and avoid its upheavals. Instead, we cultivate awareness of Orisa's work in every moment. We pay closer attention to the many opportunities for healing and change brought to us by the complexities of Orisa. We value the indispensable role of change in maintaining balance in Creation and in our lives, even when change comes roughly.

Facing Change

Change is inevitable; that goes without saying. Most of us realize and accept that reality on some level, if only to the extent that we feel powerless to avoid and control it. Tolerating change—throwing up our hands and letting change run over us—is not the same as embracing it. And embracing change is integral to maintaining our balance during times of transition and to managing the effects of change on our lives.

Embracing change is tough work, because change always walks hand-in-hand with destruction. Change intrinsically involves both breaking down and building up—and not necessarily, or even usually, in a nice, orderly fashion. Consequently, change often leads to chaos, that unpredictable, uncontrollable, whirlwind energy that can make us feel confused, powerless, and utterly devastated. Understandably, most of us prefer to steer clear of chaos; some folks try to avoid it at all costs. Nonetheless, at its core chaos is simply another way of *ashe* expressing itself.

In the Orisa pantheon, Oya is the goddess most closely associated with chaos and sudden change. As mother of wind and air, she cleanses and renews through tornadoes, hurricanes, and violent storms. It can be quite terrifying when Olodumare sends Oya to do her work in our lives. She moves so quickly and with such intense precision that often, before we know what has happened, we've been uprooted from once solid ground and set down in a place entirely different from where we were a month, week, or day ago.

Although Oya's chaos is primarily a force for destruction, it is important to remember that many things are born of chaos and much of life emerges out of darkness. Out of the charred remains of a forest decimated by fire come shelter and nutrients for all sorts of critters and seedlings. Planets and galaxies come into being out of vast, black holes. Plants burrow their life-sustaining roots into deep, dark soil. Babies emerge from the warm, dark chambers of their mothers' wombs.

Oya's lesson is that we too—despite any appearances to the contrary—can be reborn through chaos and renewed in the generous, if frightening, hands of darkness. Some form of disruption or death, some degree of blindness and loss, always heralds rebirth and transformation. If we have the courage and will to face the darkness and learn from it, even the loss of a cherished relationship or the death of a loved one can eventually bring goodness into our lives.

Oya uses chaos to create an opportunity for rebalancing by destroying old frameworks and for reorganizing things within a new structure. This usually happens because we have been in desperate need of rebalancing but have been resisting it for fear of change and of the unknown. Sometimes Oya's chaos is Olodumare's most appropriate and effective tool for nudging us to do the work we've needed to do but tenaciously avoided. It may be that only by allowing Oya's chaos to run its course and deliver its lessons can Olodumare reveal the underlying order and beauty hidden beneath the turmoil.

Resisting this process makes for a very uncomfortable existence. The more we resist change, the more chaos we draw into our lives, forcing Olodumare to use drastic measures to move us to our next lesson. We have only to remember what the elder keepers of Yoruba tradition have always understood: When the ferocious winds of She Who Topples the Old Order with Suddenness come blowing in, we might find it a little less frightening if we recognize that Olodumare is embracing us in a larger circle of renewal and rebirth.

Knowing and trusting that Olodumare always provides a clear, focused, and healing eye at the center of any storm enables us to make each breath a prayer. This is prayer not in the conventional sense of the word but as a state of awareness, a heightened consciousness that sees all life as an expression of God's breathing.

---

7. Fatunmbi Fa'lokun, *Iba'se Orisa.*

8. Alan Jones, *Soul Making: The Desert Way of Spirituality.*

9. Iyalorisha Obalade.

10. John Mason, paraphrased from *Black Gods: Orisa Studies in the New World.*

11. Babalawo Fagbemi Fasina speaks of the Orisa as "the embodied personalities of Olodumare."

12. John Mason, *Black Gods: Orisa Studies in the New World.*

13. A phrase often used in the Religious Science philosophy.

14. Another phrase often used in the Religious Science philosophy.

Chapter 3

With Every Breath

There is so much beauty in the world. Yet, most of us pass by much of it without a glance, because life has become almost unbearably busy. We rush from the moment we wake up until we fall into bed utterly depleted at the end of a long day, which inevitably is not long enough. It seems life keeps asking more from us, as we become less able to keep up with the demand. Technology has simplified many areas of our lives, while greatly complicating others. We drive ourselves mercilessly, consumed by a frenzied quest to meet our basic obligations. Then, having compromised our ability to take loving care of ourselves, we seek replenishment and respite by self-medicating. We take drugs or alcohol, binge on sugar and food, have sex for the wrong reasons, watch too much television, spend money beyond our means, or bury ourselves even further in work. Still, we remain bereft of the nourishment of God's beauty and life's joy.

The spiritual practice of breathing with God can provide a small but firm toehold against those rushing tides of over-activity that assault us. Committing to this practice means making space in our lives for beauty and recognizing beauty in places we are not used to seeing it. In sharing God's breath, we experience joy in every way we can. We learn to find splendor we might have overlooked: a contented cat curled in an apartment window, the warm May sun caressing our shoulders, a friend's smile, a stranger's kindness, the lovely face of an elderly neighbor, the majesty of old buildings, the delicate blades of grass impossibly pushing their way through a crack in the sidewalk.

The better able I am to engage in the simple act of taking notice, the fuller I am with God's breath. The more aware I am of what is happening around me, the more I train my eye to catch sight of God's hidden radiance, the more brilliance I see. In Orisa, we notice God's exquisite breath by learning to understand the language of God as it is spoken to us through Creation. Things and people become more than what they appear to be. Conversations overheard on the train become messages. Colors become signs. People we encounter become reflections of divine guidance, placed in our path to remind, teach, and show us the wonder and the way.

What most strengthens our capacity to notice God's breath is simply the intention to do so. Intending to be aware builds awareness. Awareness of God's glory can also emerge from our willingness to experience the full range of emotions within us, including pain. Sometimes the more deeply we allow pain to cut into us, the greater our capacity for beauty and joy. The ability to breathe in God's beauty is cultivated gradually over time. What opens the way is our intention. Orisa followers fortify this intention with meditation and prayer, putting aside time each day or week to practice simple awareness and to give thanks to God.

But how do we do this? How do we look beyond our pain so that we might take greater notice of God everywhere always? How do we shoulder our burdens so that we might see God's goodness all around us and let it flow into and through us? How do we tune out the noise, so we can make each moment a prayer? How do we pay homage to the deities in their multitude of forms? How do we maintain a steady awareness of Orisa and their *ashe* in all things in those rare moments of crystal clarity, let alone with every single breath?

It can be done—but usually, not without a great deal of struggle and the proper perspective. At least that has been true of my life.

This Too Is God

The truth is, part of me wants to breathe with God because I hope it will bring some sort of blissful spiritual state that will somehow raise me above my human condition. I long for a miracle spiritual pill, an easy way out of discomfort. I keep my fingers crossed that holding an awareness of Orisa as ever-present will eliminate all my doubt, tension, anxiety, and fear.

It doesn't. I don't automatically feel better just because I've opened myself to seeing God in the moment and feeling God in my breath. Remembering that God and I breathe together does not necessarily make me breathe easier. And it does not necessarily take away my anger, sadness, or grief. It doesn't put me out of reach of life's troubles. What realigning my breath with God *does* do is open me to a larger truth and bring me closer to the deities.

It is easy to be aware of life's *ashe* and to feel close to Orisa when I see their beauty and goodness radiating around me, when I feel blessed, joyful, healed, or inspired by something or someone. When I feel good, when I'm centered, and when I'm in touch with my blessings, I notice Orisa and their *ashe* everywhere. But when I am depressed or angry or sad or afraid or insecure, nothing feels like God's *ashe*. When crisis hits or when I'm faced with a situation I don't want to deal with, I usually forget all about breathing with God. In those moments of forgetfulness, as a harsh wind catches my breath and keeps me from taking in sacred energy, my life doesn't feel like God or prayer. It just feels lousy. That challenging person or situation in front of me doesn't bear the face of the gods and doesn't call me into awareness of the breath of Olodumare. Instead, I get lost in the details of whatever drama is unfolding and lose touch with my sense of Orisa and their omnipresent *ashe*.

So, whenever the shadows of my life move to the foreground, I try to turn to a concept my mother introduced me to: "this too," the Buddhist practice of approaching each moment as part of life's sacred tapestry. I say to myself, *This too is Orisa, this too is ashe*, and something shifts inside me—not necessarily away from distress, but rather toward heightened awareness. This awareness reminds me that all the beauty and divine complexities of the celestial realm and nature are also being enacted on a smaller scale in every part of my life as well as in the lives of everyone around me.

The evolutional forces at work in my life—the activity and movement of Orisa and *ashe*—parallel those at work in nature. Mountain ranges slowly rise from the earth, just as Obatala slowly cultivates humility and patience in my life. I can be volcanic with erupting anger, like Aganyu spewing hot lava. Or I can be gently flowing waters, a reflection of Oshun's tenderness. All states of being are manifestations of Orisa working in the world and our lives. Stormy waters sometimes rush onto the shores of all our lives. Every now and then, our unstable cliffs can use the healing forces of erosion, taking a little sand from here and redepositing it there, and in the process, reshaping us. Periodically, some part of our interior ecology moves out of balance, but eventually swings back into sync again.

That is exactly as it should be—ebb and flow, building up and tearing down, constantly balancing, unbalancing, and rebalancing. Such is the cycle of life, day after day, year in and year out: change, change, and more change. We cannot ask Divine Law to make allowances for us, to exempt us from struggle, simply because do not want to accept discomfort as a pathway to transformation. We can only hope that through life's changes, by making and learning from our mistakes and by striving to acknowledge "this too" as God, we are continually, if gradually, healing, unfolding, and growing.

Mindfulness

My mother, a Buddhist and daily meditator, has also given me a powerful example of how to work to enhance my consciousness of God. The purpose of her meditation is to remain focused on her breath, on the physical movement of air flowing in and out of her nostrils. This sounds simple enough. But the mind is constantly busy, forever thinking and planning. In the course of a one-hour sitting, my mom frequently gets lost in the distracting web of ceaseless mental activity and loses track of her breath, as one thought leads to another, then another, and another.

My mother accepts that in her practice she will lose focus on her breathing. She knows even after fifteen years of daily sitting that she will definitely get caught up in some story line in her mind about what's going on at work, the new curtains she wants for the living room, or some issue she's having with her kids. That is okay. She doesn't worry when her attention strays a little, because she knows she can bring it back. What she values is the process of realizing she has become distracted and of immediately returning to the breath, which might happen as many as sixty times in as many seconds.

In our quest to transform our breathing into prayers, Orisa devotees will encounter our own version of this fluctuating process of distraction and return, of closing our eyes to God and reopening them. However, I don't know whether we ever fully achieve this ability. When I look at my own life, I see that as much as I want to be an ever-mindful, constantly breathing-with-God priestess of Orisa, I am inconsistent, forgetful, and unseeing in many ways. My commitment to try to breathe with God serves as an essential guide, a vital anchor reminding me of where my work should be centered. In honesty though I don't know whether I will ever get to the point where paying conscious homage to life's many sacred faces is as automatic, constant, and involuntary as my body's process of inhaling and exhaling air. Even so, I can work toward and aspire to that goal. I can attempt to see God in myself and in others as often as I possibly can.

Maybe mastery is not what is important here anyway. Maybe forgetfulness and imperfection in these ways are just part of being human. Maybe accepting this imperfection as part of our divine makeup, as part of what makes us holy, is one way of acknowledging that *ashe* is *ashe*, whatever its manifestation. Like the Buddhists in their meditation, maybe what is most important is that we are willing to practice with humility and diligence, flexibility and intention.

Buddhists believe that perfection is illusionary and irrelevant. What matters is the moment. The purpose is not to perfect meditation but simply to practice it because practicing keeps us awake to the present, or in Yoruba terms, to God's *ashe*. Perhaps then our task is to try, but not too hard, and to approach the process as well as ourselves with compassion and humor. Perhaps the goal is to commit to doing our best and returning as often as we can to the breath of Olodumare within us. Perhaps it is enough to be aware that *ashe* and Orisa are the truth about who and what we all are, even if we are not always able to act on that awareness.

Cool Head

The Orisa reveal all sides of life to us, and we are taught to honor and embrace the contrasting, sometimes opposing, facets of any being, thing, or situation. Our tradition also recognizes the value of the middle road—the importance of staying balanced between life's extremes. Our teachings say that the clearest, most favorable route through life's rocky terrain is the road of "coolness." We call this *ori tutu* (cool headedness), the path that is neither too hot nor too cold.

We should, however, always approach this concept from a wider perspective that allows for paradox. Within the greater *both/and* view of Yoruba tradition, the concept of *ori tutu* presumes that cultivating a cool head does not necessarily mean we can or should avoid those life lessons that periodically necessitate our visits to the lands of hot and cold. Our effort to walk with *ori tutu* might lessen the impact of life's furnaces and freezing temperatures, and it might decrease the frequency with which we encounter those extremes, but it does not exempt us entirely. Working with *ori tutu* certainly doesn't mean depriving ourselves of valuable experiences for the sake of staying cool.

A cool head does not run from the heat of chaos. Rather, *ori tutu* faces chaos with equanimity. A cool head knows it has the resources it needs to ride out the storm if need be and then to restore what has been left behind, provided it warrants restoration. Those of cool head seek to understand what role they might have played in creating the situation at hand. A cool head reaches for compassion, accepts personal responsibility, and understands that coolness does not mean cutting off emotion or deadening experience.

My relationship with Orisa has taught me that no matter how sincerely I work at cultivating *ori tutu,* if I am living fully, my life will always in some way reflect the dynamic rhythms and diverse energies of Orisa—whether I like it or not, whether it's comfortable or not. Making each breath a prayer means honoring and understanding that within me Ogun's introspective nature and need for solitude coexists with Shango's loudness and passion for dancing. Oshun, mother of sweet things, lives in me as both an addictive personality prone to excess and as a mermaid who loves lipstick and low-cut dresses. Yemaya in me can be unyielding as well as giving, one day impatient and easily irritated, the next day calm and soothing.

Just as the Orisa manifest in so many forms on Earth—as nature and its cycles—so too do they manifest within each of us. Both Orisa and people are complex and multifaceted, subject to all the ways of being that go along with multiplicity. Yoruba mythology contains countless stories of Orisa making poor choices, getting into difficult situations, being moody, learning hard lessons, and generally struggling with their existence. If Olodumare does not exempt even Her own children from the challenging elements of their experiences, why should we expect our lives to be any different?

When I look at it that way, the spiritual discipline of breathing with God becomes a minute-by-minute practice of reminding myself that I am part of an interconnected web of sacred manifestation and that God is alive in all things. This approach rings more true and is more useful than my sentimental notion of chasing some unattainable, carefree spiritual bliss by walking an unwavering, totally perfect spiritual path. Looking at life and myself as perfect imperfections and nonetheless sacred becomes an invitation to see the true nature of all things as Olodumare's gift of *ashe*, given unconditionally in many unique and sometimes challenging forms. That view makes me want to at least try, whether the air is fragrant or foul, to breathe with God in every moment.

Working from Within

Some people would rather not breathe with God in every moment, preferring to take in only the pleasant breaths. I include myself in this category much of the time.

Certain folks would rather not learn from chaos, nor look for the face of Orisa in life's troubles. They often contend that the best way to coexist with the unpleasant energies life sometimes brings is to predict and control them through divination, magic, and ritual sacrifice. The problem with this approach is that many of the troubles we seek to dispel through these means have a divine purpose. Either they bring important lessons we need to learn in order to grow in some crucial way, or they show how our poor choices have made us vulnerable to disorder and crisis.

It is important for Orisa devotees to learn the rituals for directing energy, cleansing, and restoring balance, and for invoking, honoring, thanking, and utilizing sacred forces. The magic and sacrificial rites associated with Yoruba divination and healing practices are particularly potent and beautiful, and definitely have their place in our practice. But we must remember that our rituals are meant to enhance our intimacy with God, not replace it. They are not intended to provide us with tricks for getting what we want when we want it.

Ritual knowledge and skill should not be acquired like sports trophies. What is most important is not what we know, but how wisely, compassionately, and humbly we use our knowledge. Unfortunately, many Orisa devotees either misuse or overuse our ritual tools. This typically occurs when people are trying to avoid the consequences of their own actions or to apply a bandage to a situation without going to its root cause.

Some practitioners, despite their frequent ritual sacrifices and activity, live lonely, fear-ridden, and unfulfilled lives. They may cast the oracle every day, and it may provide them with a steady flow of ritual prescriptions for averting potential disaster or manifesting desired outcomes. They may perform sacrifice upon sacrifice for the sake of keeping their roads clear of whatever misfortune or debris they may think is out there. In the meantime, however, they neglect to attend to the spiritual and emotional debris that we all carry within. Ritual only partially clears up all that internal stuff, which we can only cleanse completely by taking care of and working on ourselves. In the right hands, our oracles and ceremonies facilitate profound healing and blessings, but they can never guarantee our peace, well-being, or joy. They will not fix our lives. Ritual and sacrifice can never eliminate the need for looking within, for courageously facing what we see there, and for taking the necessary actions to heal and change.

We invite much more into our lives, good or bad, than we realize. That does not mean we always recognize and welcome these catalysts, or even that we're aware of the connection between them (cause) and us (effect). Though we may not consciously create a situation, we might enable it by living unconsciously. Unacknowledged pain, buried fears, unrealistic expectations, and false beliefs can generate negative life patterns and circumstances. By the same token, walking through life unaware can prevent us from realizing the gifts that come to us as well as those within us. We may also experience the effects of something that happened so long ago—perhaps in childhood or even before our current lifetimes—that we cannot distinguish the source from the outcome.

Sometimes it is not ours to know or control, at least initially and certainly not alone without God's involvement. We can be awake to our lives, working consciously to attract and embrace positive experiences and to repel or dispel negative ones, and still things happen and affect us in ways we cannot predict or understand. When we hit a rough patch, it doesn't necessarily mean we chose the path that led us there. It could be that we need to walk a certain hard road in order to learn some lesson Olodumare wants for us. It could also be that the sacred purpose behind that challenge is to provide a lesson or healing to others.

Every human experience has a sacred purpose, which may or may not reveal itself or even manifest during our lifetimes. Sacred forces are constantly at work, guiding us to, away from, and through every leg of our earthly journey. However, we must remember that we co-create our lives in partnership with God. We should not presume that all suffering is avoidable and without benefit. Nor should we expect prayer and ritual to spare us every pain and challenge and to draw every joy and reward into our lives.

When we seek to resolve all our obstacles and to attract all our riches through magic and ritual alone, we end up missing the point: Life is a teacher and as students we have a responsibility to pay close attention to Orisa's lessons and to actively participate in co-creating our lives. For in truth, both loss and gain bring us precious opportunities for deepening our souls. Every moment we make choices, both consciously and unconsciously, that shape our experience for better or worse. Often what we think we want is contrary to the lesson or healing that Orisa has in mind for us.

That is why it is important not only to turn to the gods when we need help getting through hard times, but also to give thanks for the ways hard times reshape us and for the blessings the resulting transformation brings. We should develop the habit of looking back at the struggles we've come through and of making ritual to celebrate the Orisa's role in guiding us through those struggles. We should give thanks to Olodumare, whose larger plan for us is unfolding gradually in ways that are sometimes enjoyable and sometimes painful. We should do so regularly—not out of obligation or for fear of angering or disappointing God—but with sincerity and pure intention. We should expect nothing in return, graciously accepting the gift of breathing with God in the moment.

The very nature of Creation—Olorun's essence—is a circular continuum of tears and laughter, push and pull, opening and closing, building up and tearing down. No amount of divination and sacrifice can undo or assuage certain sufferings. Some agonies are simply beyond our ability to comprehend or resolve. However, healing is not the same as curing, and it is recovery from, not eradication of, a difficult situation that replenishes and restores our souls. What we cannot fix we may still learn from and use in our continuing effort to become more evolved beings. That in itself is a blessing.

Orisa Soul Work

Try these practices for finding the beauty and the breath of God in your everyday life.

- Spend a twenty-four-hour period being as mindful as you can of the many ways in which God reveals Itself through Orisa during the course of your day.

- When crossing the threshold of your home, greet Elegua, who lives in all entryways.

- During a difficult conversation with your best friend, coworker, or lover—the one you've been putting off for weeks—remember that Ogun, guardian of truth, bestower of courage, sits right beside you.

- When you pass a pregnant woman on the street, thank Yemaya, mother of the world, for showing herself to you.

- When you go out for a night on the town, know that Oshun and Shango, the keepers of sensuality who always enjoy a good time, are celebrating with you.

- Greet Obatala in every white-haired elder you see. The color white is one of his most potent medicines, and old people are his special messengers.

- Acknowledge Oya as the air flowing around and through your body.

- Use every conversation, every circumstance, and every moment as an opportunity to see Orisa—and God. When you stray from this awareness, bring yourself gently but firmly back to the *ashe*, which is alive all around you.

- Commit yourself to this practice once a month and notice how it changes you over time.

Letting Go of Punishment

I don't know why God does what It does—why airplanes crash, why tsunamis wipe out villages, why slavery happened, and why oppression, poverty, AIDS, and other tragedies continue to devastate so many. I may never know why certain parts of my childhood had to be so painful or why certain losses have at times devastated my heart. Why Olodumare allows certain things to take place is beyond my capacity to understand. What I do know is that Elegua, guardian of the threshold, is Olodumare's servant, and when he holds open the door to disaster or misfortune, it is because Olodumare has asked him to.

We should not misconstrue this to mean that Olodumare or the Orisa are vengeful—even though there is, unfortunately, a strong punitive undercurrent in Orisa tradition. Followers of this approach tend to teach and live by fear, to see the wrath of the gods in every struggle, challenge, and unfortunate situation. Whenever something bad happens, they are quick to judge and assign blame: someone has done something wrong and is being fittingly punished for it.

When seen through this kind of punitive lens, all of life's troubles seem like retribution from God for some wrong or slight committed. In truth, when bad things happen, more often than not the causes and reasons behind them are much more complicated. The Orisa operate on many levels more complex than that. As guardians of natural law, they exist in our lives to help us embrace the life paths that are ours by destiny. They are not here to criticize or punish us. They do not watch our every move, waiting for us to mess up so they can visit harm upon us.

What will hurt us is filling our lives with too much fear and stress and not enough nurturing. What gets us in trouble is allowing some truth to fester until it knocks our lives out of balance, demanding attention. The unhealthy ways we go about our relationships, our toxic emotional patterns and addictions—these will break us down. We always pay for our unacknowledged self-loathing, unhealed childhood issues, and unresolved baggage. When we can no longer suppress our unexpressed anger and unforgiven hurts, they emerge as bitter hearts or disease, causing more damage. Soul agreements we carry over from previous lifetimes will catch up with us. Silence and denial of our true feelings, thoughts, and needs will stifle us. Our misaligned priorities, our inability to apologize, and our fear of change will harm us. The choices we make to make things easier at whatever price will cost us.

I do not believe God punishes us for the choices we make. But I definitely know we have to live with the results of those choices. It isn't Olodumare's disapproval or for that matter Her approval that we must consider. We receive divine love and forgiveness unconditionally.[15] Both are given freely whenever we move past our ignorance and fear, let go of our attachment to image, and turn toward God. What we have to account for are the lives we are creating and whether we acknowledge and learn from our mistakes.

When we are unwilling to push beyond our limitations and comfort zones, we end up treating ourselves far more ruthlessly than God in the natural order of things ever does. This shows up in chaotic and distressing ways, and can be extremely painful. But when something agonizing or drastic happens in our lives, does it mean divine retribution is at hand? When Elegua, master change-maker, brings us loss and suffering, is he mad and disciplining us for not being good? Or is he simply bringing crisis to our door to shake things up a little, to open our eyes to the ways we've been sleepwalking and not taking care of ourselves? Is it possible that Elegua wants to make way for change that is ultimately for our greater good? I believe so.

This approach is far more conducive to our soul's learning than the fire and brimstone model, which may keep us in line, but won't necessarily help us live more deeply. The Orisa do not punish so much as they restore balance. They are more concerned with healing than with blaming. Because God's pervasive desire is for us to be restored to wholeness, the universe will periodically expose the places in us that need looking at so that we can pay attention to and mend them. God is not trying to punish us; God is trying to enrich us.

What we might call the wrath of the gods is sometimes really the divine law of cause and effect in action, because everything we think, believe, say, or do has power and influences our experience, relationships, and evolution. Every act and inability to act, every conscious or unconscious decision, impacts how we perceive and what we receive from life. Every cause generates a corresponding effect. Every effect has a divine function in our lives.

Of course, we must take into consideration that our personal experiences exist within the context of society and its systems over which we as individuals have little power. Still, while we may have minimal control over the ways in which these institutional forces define external conditions in our lives, we can control how we choose to react to those conditions. We can choose to participate in these destructive forces, to support them through our inaction and silence, or to combat them with intention and action. To free ourselves from societal shackles, we must rid ourselves of the habitual responses Bob Marley called "mental slavery." We can train ourselves to respond to oppressive outer conditions in ways that bring benefit rather than harm to us and others. Likewise, we can choose to fear God and call the tragedies and hardships that come to us punishment, or we can choose to learn as much as we can from everything that God and life bring us.

Bittersweet Divine Mystery

I believe it is Creation's natural impulse to nourish and nurture. I believe that Olorun, Olodumare, and the Orisa are fundamentally loving energies. Yet, the law of cause and effect as well as the interdependent relationship between light and dark are also fundamental to Creation.

The reasons bad things happen to good people[16] may be far more complex than I can make sense of. There are surely mysteries in life I cannot decipher, times when I cannot explain how bitterness can coexist with tenderness. For example, I know that many of my ancestors suffered profoundly on the journey through the Middle Passage and that those who survived were then subjected to the humiliation and violence of slavery. I know it, and I see the effects of it every day—in my family and in the lives of other black people I've known.

Yet, it is across this same waterway that the Orisa made their way during the diaspora. It is because ancestors in my spiritual lineage were stolen away from their loved ones that my elders, first in Cuba and then in New York, were given the abundant spiritual treasure that they eventually passed on to me. It is the slave trade that brought our tradition out of Africa so that centuries later you and I could be the beneficiaries of these teachings. My *both/and* Yoruba mind knows I must struggle to hold on to these two opposing sides, as irreconcilable as they may seem, for therein lies many of my life's truths.

In our search for the soul of the Orisa path we will from time to time face some challenging complexities. The experiences that Orisa brings us may not always make sense. We may not be able to solve every problem and every mystery. We may find ourselves asking, *Why me? Why this? Why now?*

We may not understand why life sometimes suddenly turns on us when we least expect it and feel completely unprepared to deal with it.

As practitioners of this tradition, it is both our challenge and our blessing to awaken to the many rhythms, colors, textures, and sounds of *ashe* as it moves through our lives. Learning to make each breath a prayer is hard but joyful work. Through our efforts to become aware of the *ashe* in ourselves and everything we see, hear, and touch, we discover—if only fleetingly—what it feels like to breathe as God breathes. The key is to trust that every hardship in life bears the gift of learning and that religion alone cannot answer all questions. Orisa teaches us to embrace the fundamental mystery of life and to seek the face of God in all things.

---

15. My dear friend Saidiya Hartman spoke eloquently of this concept one afternoon over tea, and I have borrowed from her words here.

16. Harold Kushner, *When Bad Things Happen to Good People*.

PART TWO

GARDEN OF THE SPIRITS

To get to the soul of Orisa, we begin with the *egun*, the ancestors. The Yoruba believe that the spirits of our ancestors walk among us. Having shed physical form, they continue to function on Earth as powerful forces that bring healing and good to the living. The Yoruba also believe that the living give longevity to the dead. We keep them alive through our memories of them, and their energies and genetic imprints on our souls shape who we are and how we live our lives. The living and the dead are inextricably woven together in a sacred tapestry of interrelatedness. We exist in different places on the same continuum. We belong to a single story.

Part two of this book focuses on the ancestors' part in this story and the process of opening ourselves to our *egun*. There are no instructions here for memorizing the proper prayers or for performing the right rituals; that information must be passed from elder to student. Instead, I will talk here about the process of developing a substantive, intimate, day-to-day connection with the ancestors. We will look at how to approach the spirits in a way that allows them to become a wellspring of divine blood that is as vital to your soul as the blood coursing through your veins is to your body.

Orisa teachings say that the nearest resolution to any problem resides with the spirits of your bloodline. As my godfather, Cyril "Skip" Butler-Omitolukun, says, "If we think we see farther, it is only because we are standing on the shoulders of those who came before us." In Orisa, every *mojuba*, or formal prayer, begins by first honoring the ancestors, the holy Mothers and Fathers.[1] All ritual work directed at the deities proceeds in similar fashion, by first invoking and thanking the spirits.

Any elder you choose to learn from will start you on the path of Orisa by first making sure your feet are firmly planted in the soil of the ancestors. Working in the ancestral garden will become fundamental to your daily life and will provide the foundation upon which you learn to breathe with God. In order to know the deities, you must first know yourself, which involves knowing intimately and paying homage to your roots, your origins, the *egun*.

Cultivating a soulful connection with *egun* requires our full commitment, focused attention, hard work, and consistent care. As we do the daily, often heart-wrenching and back-breaking work of turning over, seeding, weeding, and tending the ancestral garden, the rhythms of our lives start to change. When we learn to share our existence with a palpable and wise spiritual presence, our relationship with the *egun* becomes a sheltering arm that protects us when we are vulnerable, embraces us when we are lonely, and carries us when we are too weak to walk alone.

Gradually we learn how to give our plot the right balance of light and water and how to protect it from the spiritual predators of fear and soulless ritual. We develop the ability to work gently through difficult feelings about those ancestors whose actions when alive caused harm to us or our loved ones. We discover spiritual resources for tending to the unmourned losses and unhealed rages within our family histories, those tangled vines that live alongside the succulent vegetation in all lineages. With work and in time, we find ourselves in an abundant garden overflowing with sweet fruit to sustain us on our journeys and strengthened by the vital roots out of which our existence has sprung.

It takes years to grow a lush ancestral garden, to discover which fruits grow well beside which vegetables, which rituals and practices will strengthen your bond with the *egun*. It takes continual practice to discern which parts of your plot are loamy, sandy, clay, and rocky and how best to enrich each. You'll need certain tools, materials, and basic information. I give them to you here as my elders gave them to me and as I have learned to work with them in caring for my own garden of the spirits. Make them your own and work with them as your heart tells you.

Chapter 4

The Ancestral Shrine

The most essential tool for growing communion with the *egun* is the ancestral shrine, the *oju egun* (literally, "face of the ancestors" in Yoruba). In Orisa, the *oju egun* is vital to all spiritual journeys: people of any ethnicity or religion can benefit from tending to and working with an ancestral altar.

Yoruba altars, or shrines, fall into two broad categories: those dedicated to the spirits and those dedicated to the gods. One of the first steps of any *aborisha* (Orisa priest or priestess) is assisting their new *omo* (student; literally, "child" in Yoruba) in opening a shrine for the ancestors. The shrine becomes a gathering place for the spirits who live on in our midst as potent energy, still part of the family.

A Yoruba proverb states: *Iyen èwo se yega àwon wá saájú ghon waalé:* "That which made for the success of those who came before must be noted by those who come after."[2] The *egun* altar gives us a place to acknowledge the achievements and attributes, as well as the sorrows and struggles, of our ancestors. It lets our ancestors know we want a deeper connection with them and invites them into the fabric of our daily lives. The shrine creates a focal point in the material realm where our spirits can gather to witness our prayers and rituals in their honor. It provides a means of harmonizing their energies with ours. It is a gesture of love and respect that says to our spirits, "We want you here. We value your presence. And so we have put aside a special place devoted to you."

One important function of the *egun* shrine is to provide a sacred physical area for remembering those spirits whose lives were brutalized by some form of atrocity, such as slavery or genocide. These ancestors, many of whom may be experiencing difficulty finding peace in the spirit world, have an especially strong desire to be remembered by the living. Most of the items that go on an *egun* shrine are elevatory in nature and will provide some help to these spirits.

Sometimes, however, a person's bloodline is so tangled, occupied by spirits who are so distressed and out of balance, that elevating those spirits requires more than simply keeping a shrine. In fact, under those circumstances, approaching the *egun* directly could be detrimental to the practitioner's well-being. If that is your situation—and most people know when it is, either by outward signs or by gut feelings—this part of the book is not for you. I urge you, instead, to seek the skilled assistance of an elder who can give your troubled ancestors the light they need, so you can then safely begin to work with them. If you don't have access to a Yoruba elder, a qualified spiritualist can perform the work necessary to quiet agitated *egun* so that you can work with them safely and effectively.

There is no single set of directions for setting up an *egun* shrine. Orisa practitioners honor their ancestors in a variety of inspired and beautiful ways, none more correct than any others. For example, many Orisa initiates practice the powerful and lovely Mesa Blanca tradition, which takes a slightly different approach to keeping an ancestral altar than the one given here. Many elements of Mesa Blanca were incorporated into the way I was taught and continue to inform the way I work today. However, Mesa Blanca cannot be learned from a book, whereas simple guidelines for welcoming the ancestors into your daily life can, and that is what I provide here.

This how-to information will be most relevant to people who are not working with an elder. If you are part of an *ile* (religious house, community, family, or temple), you will obviously want to follow the instructions of your godparents. For everyone else, use the following as a guide for setting up and working with your altar. Take only what feels right for you. Don't hesitate to follow your intuition; the ancestors often speak through hunches and gut feelings, and those instincts will rarely mislead you.

Setting Up an *Egun* Altar

You will want to reserve a place for your altar in a comfortable room in your home where you can sit with the spirits whenever and however you want. At different times, I have set up an *egun* shrine in the living room, the dining room, near where I write, in the kitchen, and even in the bathroom.

Some people don't want others to see their shrines and keep them out of sight, behind closed doors or in locked cabinets. Others may want visitors to see the ancestral shrine first thing when they walk in the door. Whether you keep your shrine in a secluded or open space depends upon your living arrangement, with whom you share your home, and what makes you feel most at ease. Your shrine can be on any open surface or behind closed doors. It can go against a wall, in a corner, or in the center of a room. Where you set up your altar is entirely up to you; just give it a place that feels respectful to the spirits and right for you.

Most elders say you shouldn't put your ancestors in the bedroom or where you have sex. It is not that sex is bad; in fact, Yoruba teachings say just the opposite. It is just that having sex in front of your shrine is like making love in front of your grandparents; it's not something you'd want to do. If you live in a small space and need to share your bedroom with *egun*, put a screen of some sort in front of them before you have sex.

Wherever you put your shrine, make sure the people who share or visit your home understand that the shrine is a sacred place and that they are not to pick up or touch the objects on it. Every altarpiece is enlivened with the energy of the ancestor it represents, and it reflects the personal relationship you'll be developing with that spirit.

To set up a basic ancestor shrine the way I was taught by my godmother requires a few simple items: a table, a vessel of water, a white cloth, and a white candle. Most altars should also include the names and photographs of your dead family members, but these are optional. Include them only if they are available to you and relevant to your spiritual needs.

You can use a table of any shape and size—or anything with a flat surface, such as a shelf, bureau top, or even a footstool. Make sure the altar table or platform is clean, cleared of all other objects, and stable.

Alternatively, you can keep *egun* on the bare floor, adjacent to a wall or corner. Draw a semicircle on the floor with *cascarilla* (a chalk-like powdered eggshell) or with *efun* (crushed snail shell or African clay). Draw nine vertical lines at even intervals along the curved line of the semicircle; each line must slash through the semicircle, like a child's drawing of the sun. Nine is the sacred number of the ancestors. The semicircle graphically separates the world of the spirits (within the circle) from the world of the living (outside the circle). The nine lines connect the two realms and represent the *egun's* role as rays of light in our lives.

In a corner

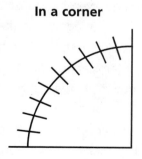

Against a wall

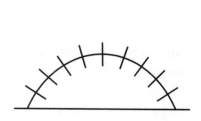

Cover the surface of the table or whatever you choose to form the base of your altar with a white cloth, preferably cotton, which comes from the same earth to which the bones and flesh of the ancestors have returned. The color white is important, because it visually reflects light around your shrine and attracts energy, clarity, and peace to spirits who may need elevation. Anything white on your altar will help lift, pacify, and comfort spirits in need.

Keep clean water in a clear glass vase or a large glass goblet on your altar, preferably in the center. I suggest using clear, uncut glass to ensure clear, unfiltered transmission between you and your spirits. Water is basic to all life and serves several functions on your altar. Giving water to the ancestors challenges the supposed finality of death, by acting as a medium, providing a conduit for communication between you and the spirits. It also cleanses, harmonizes, and balances the energies around your shrine, bringing those qualities to any spirits who might need them.

You'll also want to burn white candles for the ancestors. The safest are tall, seven-day candles encased in glass, but you can also use votives, tapers, and even inexpensive utility candles. White candlelight is like a magnet for the dead and will draw them to the shrine. However, I wouldn't burn a white candle in any space unfamiliar to you until you're sure the spirits who will be drawn to the light are healthy and balanced.

Photographs or illustrations of your ancestors can help you feel more connected to them. Just make sure you put only images of the dead on the altar. If you are especially attached to a photo of you and your deceased grandmother, you'll need to cut yourself out of the picture before placing it on the shrine. Although you are making space in your world for the spirits, it is important to remember that the space you are providing for them is a contained one and that they live in their world and you live in yours. Though it is all right for these worlds to intersect through the *egun* shrine, they should never merge.

You can also make a list of your ancestors' names in descending order from the eldest (or longest dead) to the youngest. You can be simple or creative with this, using fancy calligraphy to write the names or simply printing them from your computer—whatever feels right to you. The list is especially useful if you don't have photos of your *egun* but know their names. For my altar I usually keep one long list on a single sheet of paper. You could also write individual names on small separate strips of paper placed on the table or strung like a necklace and hung on or above your altar.

There are several other traditional and unique altar-pieces you can use to summon and honor the spirits. Many people keep dirt or artifacts from their ancestors' homelands on their shrines. If you have personal items that belonged to your ancestors, you can keep those on the altar as well.

You might want to bring flowers to your *egun*, especially sweet-smelling ones, white or any color. My elder, Obalade, uses carnations, which she calls absorbent, to pull negative energies out of the environment. Perfume, cologne, or scented oil on the altar can also serve as a beacon to draw the *egun* out of their world and to your altar. Use something you like but don't actually wear; your spirits will come to recognize this as your spiritual "smell."

As soon as you've put together your altar, begin sharing food with your ancestors. At every meal before you serve the living members of your household, put a few bites from each dish on the shrine for the spirits, so they can partake of the same nourishment you do. Sharing food has always been a way of bringing people together; it fulfills the same purpose between the spirits and the living. I shop at thrift stores for teacups and saucers that I use exclusively for this purpose. You can use any dish or container you want for your *egun* food offerings, but to protect the boundary between the two worlds, never feed the *egun* with the dishes you use to feed the living.

Once you've set up the basic shrine, you can add offerings that please the spirits as you discover them. Tobacco, coffee, and rum are common offerings on ancestral shrines. Rum calls your *egun* to attention, alerting them to the altar's presence and you to theirs. Some spirits like it if you pour or spit the rum directly onto the floor in front of the shrine. Coffee—usually black with sugar, but cream is fine if you know one of your ancestors liked it that way—invigorates the connection between you and your ancestors. Tobacco has healing powers, and for more advanced practitioners, it is used to induce trance. It is best to use a cigar, hand-rolled cigarette, pipe, or loose tobacco belonging to or similar to the one used by your ancestor. Unless a spirit asks for it (as my grandmother, a chain-smoker, did), I would avoid using packaged cigarettes, because of their filters and other unnatural ingredients.

Be flexible and sensible about how you adorn this space. Choose only items that have good energy and spiritual relevance, and work with what you have or can easily get. For example, I don't have any pictures of my father's grandparents, but I know the name of the small town in east Texas where they lived more than a hundred years ago. So, when I was driving across the United States with my sister, I took a picture of the two-lane road that runs through this part of rural east Texas and the sign beside it, which reads, "Arp, Population 812." I keep this photo on my altar to represent that strand of my lineage.

Do not place things on the altar simply because you like them or think they look nice. Add only those altarpieces the spirits want. Usually, when something catches our attention and a little voice says, *Put that on the shrine*, it is a message from an ancestor who wants it there as some sort of medicine or tool. But every now and then we may be mistaken, so it is a good idea to always check first with your *egun*. Your elder can assist with the divination process used for this purpose. If you are not an Orisa devotee but have access to a divination system that can supply you with yes/no answers, use it to ask your spirits if they want a particular item before you add it. If you don't have access to a divination tool, just meditate on it and trust your intuition.

Egun Shrine Essentials

Your *oju egun* will be a dynamic and very personal place of worship that develops as your relationship with the ancestors develops. As the faces of your spirits reveal themselves to you and as you reveal yours to them, you will discover things you want to add or remove from the altar. You can start with these essential altarpieces:

Table. A small table or flat surface dedicated to this purpose. Alternatively, you can draw an altar space (a semicircle with nine intersecting lines) on the floor.

White cloth. To cover the table. (Obviously, if you create an altar on the floor, you wouldn't cover it with a white cloth.)

Water. Clean water kept in a clear, uncut glass vessel. Place at the center of the altar.

White candle. One of any type, to start. Place at or near the center of the altar.

Family photos. Photographs, drawings, or paintings of dead family members, if available.

Ancestors' names. The names of all your relatives, on a list on a piece of paper, or on many small pieces of paper.

Artifacts. Dirt or artifacts from your *egun*'s homeland or any personal item belonging to a relative.

Flowers. Fresh-cut or potted flowers, any color, preferably scented.

Scent. Any perfume, cologne, or scented oil that fits your spiritual essence but that you don't wear in your everyday life.

Food. A tiny portion of everything you eat and drink, offered daily on plates used exclusively for this purpose.

Tobacco. To please or heal an ancestor.

Rum and coffee. To stimulate and "warm" the connection between you and the spirits.

Consecrating the Altarpieces

You should clean anything you add to your shrine to prepare it for its sacred purpose. Consecration purifies and blesses the altarpiece and enlivens it with the energy needed to connect you with your ancestors. If you don't have an elder to perform the consecration ritual with you, you can consecrate altar items yourself in various ways: by rubbing them with herbs, blowing cigar smoke on them, immersing them in sea salt, or burning sage or frankincense.

When in doubt, use what in Orisa tradition is considered to be the most potent, magical power for blessing—water. Cool, fresh tap water is fine. Water is imbued with the powers to heal and refresh. It is also particularly responsive to speech. Words spoken over water with reverence and clear intention become a powerful force for changing the mind, body, energy, and emotions.

To consecrate an altarpiece with water:

- Pour water into a clay or glass bowl.
- Pray over the bowl, speaking directly into the water, asking for whatever you seek.
- Close your prayer by saying, "And so it is."
- Sprinkle the object with water or immerse it in the bowl.

Initiated Orisa practitioners will probably want to do more elaborate consecrations, according to what their elders have taught them.

Keep your shrine clean and free of dust, moldy food, and murky liquids. Since water conducts energy and supports the clear flow of relationship between you and your ancestors, the water on your shrine must be kept fresh. Change your water at least once every nine days or whenever it starts to get cloudy.

Periodically—if the spirits have asked for it—you may want to rearrange your altar. For example, you might feel the need to move the shrine to another table or room, to reposition the water vessel, or to make the altar bigger. Just as you will add altarpieces based on the ancestors and issues you are working on at a given time, so you can also remove an object after it has served its purpose—once the issue or blockage has been resolved or the spirit has been elevated.

The important thing is to pay attention to what your *egun* are telling you about what they need and how you worship at the altar. What makes an ancestor shrine is the effort, heart, and intention we give it, not how many things we put on the altar or how much money we spend on it. If you have limited space or resources, don't let that stop you. Keep a clear glass of water and a white candle in a small nook, spend time there regularly, bring your ancestors food, and be yourself, and you will have as powerful an *egun* shrine as any.

---

1. Babalawo Fagbemi Fasina's term.
2. Babalawo Ifajukuta, http://ifajakuta.freeyellow.com.

Chapter 5

Growing Deep Relationships with the Ancestors

Death for the Yoruba does not mark the end of a life, but rather a fork in a soul's road. At that juncture, one passes into a different world where the body is no longer necessary and life takes form as energy. The value of the ancestral shrine is that it serves as a contact point where the material and spiritual worlds meet. Keeping an *egun* altar changes our relationship to loved ones who have passed on, allowing us to remain connected to them in our daily lives. But deepening that connection enough to elevate our troubled *egun* and to improve our own lives requires much more than merely setting up an altar and saying the occasional perfunctory prayer. It takes doing the work—praying, making ritual, and meditating—on a consistent basis, with sincerity and clear intention, sometimes in community with others, but always in our private lives.

Prayer

The Yoruba have a well-stocked repository of prayers for addressing the *egun* on just about any topic. Handed down from elder to novice, these prayers are entirely appropriate for traditional ceremonies or when your spirits ask for them. But they are not the only or necessarily the best way to worship the *egun*.

The thought of praying to one's ancestors can be intimidating, particularly to those of us who are uneasy about our past or feel uncertain about whether we are praying correctly. One of the important lessons I have learned through my Orisa practice is, there is no right way or no wrong way to pray to the ancestors. In fact, developing intimacy, trust, and a sense of ease with our *egun* often requires that we augment the more formal, traditional rituals with a looser, more personal approach to prayer. I have found that worshiping in ways that are comfortable for me and that come from the heart bring the greatest benefits.

In praying to your *egun*, don't worry if you speak a different language from the ones your ancestors spoke. They can hear beyond words to your deepest intentions. Let your personal prayers to them reflect the full range of your thoughts, emotions, and experiences. Ask for what you need and give thanks for what they've given you. Pray to express your empathy and respect for the struggles they endured. Acknowledge the gifts you have and your ancestors' roles in putting them in your life. Ask them to protect you from harm and to heal you, your family, and the world. Pay reverence to your spirits by simply spending time with them at the altar, sharing your goals and dreams. Be creative with your prayers—chant them, sing them, move your body to them, whisper or shout them, paint or sculpt them. Most important, pray with honesty and authenticity.

Making Ritual

Ritual is an essential thread running through all Yoruba practices. The Yoruba seem to have a ritual for every spiritual and human experience, from birth to death and everything in between and after. Yoruba rituals range from simple to complex. They can last for minutes or days. They might involve the entire community, an initiate and his or her elder, or the devotee alone. Whatever the nature of the ritual, its purpose is always to pay homage to the sacred nature of all life.

Ritual serves many purposes in Orisa tradition. It may be used to honor an ancestor, to calm or soothe an agitated spirit, or to align us with the *egun* of our line. Similarly, ritual is the vehicle for invoking the gods and for focusing their energies toward a specific purpose. Orisa has countless rituals for healing all sorts of physical, emotional, and spiritual imbalances. Divination and sacrifice always involve some type of ritual for directing spiritual energy toward removing or cleansing negative influences, whether internal or external, or toward harmonizing us with our highest good. Rituals involving possession, in which an Orisa priest absorbs and embodies a spiritual entity, serve much the same purpose, enabling the *egun* or deity to communicate and work more directly with us.

Most rituals geared toward contacting and communicating with the spirits take place in communal settings and require the skills of at least one spiritualist or medium. This person is responsible for channeling and regulating the energies, and for receiving and transmitting messages from the dead that provide guidance for those in attendance.

Each of the myriad traditional ceremonies has a specific divine purpose, and all are cornerstones of the tradition that must be learned at the knees of an elder. However, personal rituals that are unique to the worshiper and performed privately are equally powerful and an essential nourishment for our individual ancestral gardens. These rituals come to us through our dreams or intuitive knowing. The possibilities for private ritual are limited only by our abilities to intercept and interpret what our spirits are asking for and to find creative ways for inviting the *egun* into our daily lives.

Ritual is any reverent activity that helps us feel more connected to a sacred presence. It may consist of changing the water in your glass vase every three days or saying prayers in front of your shrine every evening before bed. It may consist of reading to your ancestors from the Bible or whatever sacred text they looked to for sustenance. You may prepare a lavish feast once a season for your *egun,* serving all their favorite foods and drinks. You may bring flowers once a week or pour fresh coffee for your *egun* every morning at sunrise.

Whatever rituals you choose, make sure you commit to doing only what fits the flow of your life. When you say you're going to do something, be consistent and follow through.

Otherwise, you may disappoint your *egun* and weaken your relationship with them.

Revisioning Appeasement

For those who are unfamiliar with the concept of appeasement, it means making certain ritual sacrifices to the ancestors or the deities to keep them happy with us or to atone for our slights or failings. Usually, it goes something like this: We go about our religious life doing the appropriate rituals and prayers. Occasionally, we neglect to perform a ritual or do it improperly, and the ancestors or deity get angry. Seeking retribution, they lash out against us by wreaking havoc in our lives. Because we've fallen out of favor with them, we attempt to win back their generosity and to restore balance in our lives by appeasing their fiery tempers with the appropriate calming rituals. Obligation rather than love and fear rather than intimacy drive the initiate.

Many practitioners have grown weary of this extreme and punitive form of appeasement. A number of us wonder whether this perform-or-be-punished view serves to protect the interests of people in power (mainly, priests) more than to satisfy the needs of the practitioner, the *egun,* and the deities. The fact that these appeasements typically require the expertise of a priest—who often gets paid handsomely for his or her services—only contributes to the growing dissatisfaction with this approach. I believe that it is time for a new, less punitive, and more restorative approach.

Traditionally, an ancestor who needs appeasing is considered dangerous. On one level that makes sense, because such a spirit is usually behaving in disturbing or destructive ways to the living, sometimes in extreme and dangerous proportion. But it is important to look beyond this reality to the wiser truth that a spirit in search of appeasement is almost always one in need of assistance. Unelevated spirits suffer from wounds they cannot heal on their own. They are disturbed and crave our understanding, not our fear. They don't want our suffering, they need our help in alleviating whatever torment or imbalance is causing their inappropriate behavior. A spirit in distress needs elevation, which enables a troubled ancestor to move out of darkness and into the light, so that it can fulfill its divine destiny as a force for helping the living.

Spirits in this condition need not present a danger to us, as long as we are equipped to deal with them. Armed with the proper knowledge and tools—or, if the situation calls for it, a qualified medium working on our behalf—we can give love, compassion, and service to a spirit who is lost and seeking peace. That doesn't mean elevating a troubled ancestor is necessarily easy or painless. It can be challenging, frightening, and sometimes beyond the initiate's abilities to deal with alone. If that is the case, don't hesitate to call in a skilled medium, who isn't afraid of *egun*, knows how to handle any situation brought on by a wayward spirit, and trusts the ancestral guides who always walk with him or her.

Once the medium has calmed your disturbed ancestor, you can resume working with them.

Relief from their own agony isn't the only reason the spirits seek appeasement. It may be their way of delivering a message we have been unable or unwilling to hear. When that happens, we can often appease them by receiving the message and taking action on it.

In working with my ancestors, intimacy and trust matter more to me than fear. Therefore, I have had to reframe the concept of appeasement into a more benevolent spiritual practice. I stay away from attitudes or practices that may bring fear and therefore hurt my relationships with my spirits. And I have adopted appeasement rituals and prayers that foster an open and constructive connection with my *egun.*

Growing a deep relationship with your ancestors will probably require you to take a fresh look at appeasement. The traditional approach thrives on fear; fear only begets more fear, and it is virtually impossible to feel close to something we are afraid of. Security and intimacy go hand in hand. If we are to bond with our ancestors, we must feel safe in their presence. When our relationship with *egun* draws too heavily from the well of fear-driven appeasement, it fills us with doubt and apprehension, which damages, rather than strengthens, our ancestral relationships. When we overly invest in the duties and obligations that so often drive a ritual life of constant appeasing, our practice loses its heart and becomes burdensome and oppressive.

Fear of ancestral vengeance will make you do things out of obligation rather than love. Fear of incurring an ancestral wrath will compel you to perform habitual and empty acts for the sake of propriety. Fear of capricious ancestral danger will consume your life energy with an endless succession of empty rituals performed simply because they are supposedly the right thing to do. None of that will help you feel more soulfully connected to your people. What will connect you is being receptive to your ancestors' needs and basing your relationship with them on mutual trust, honesty, and love.

What Right Way?

Appeasement is not the only area of our ancestral garden that we may need to rethink. Finding the soul of our ancestral connection usually also requires expanding our notion of reverence. For many of us, words like *ritual, ceremony*, and *prayer* usually imply a kind of formality, which is defined as something "perfunctory, having the form without the spirit," "done to comply with a rule," or with "stiffness of design."[3]

In the garden of the ancestors, the last thing we want is to be stiff and self-conscious, more concerned with following rules than with flowing from the soul. Although the more formal aspects of ancestral worship have a right and proper place in our spiritual lives, we must balance these with a personal form of worship that comes from the heart. Otherwise, our practice can become a shell of soulless and perfunctory behaviors that multiply like a fungus, steadily devouring the soul connection we hope to develop.

The health and vibrancy of our ancestral garden requires that we unmask our true selves, even if what we reveal conflicts with who we think we should be or must do. We must make sure we aren't overly focused on performing the right rituals and neglecting to develop intimacy with the spirits. We should also be clear and upfront about what we are asking of and from our ancestors.

Usually when people start working with an *egun* shrine, they are filled with anxiety about making a mistake or upsetting the spirits. But I find that if we approach the process with a genuine willingness to learn—and with the same respect we would show to anyone with whom we want a meaningful relationship—we are unlikely to offend our spirits. In truth, the biggest offense we can commit is to approach the spirits with pretense and fear.

Fear is a corrosive energy. If we let it, fear will destroy our relationship with the *egun.* It will kill our ancestral garden, cutting off the supply of vital nutrients to its roots, and withering our spiritual growth. If you want your garden to thrive, you'll need to work against fear. If you find it lurking, you will need to have the courage to look straight at it and listen to it carefully. Find out what it has to teach you about your heritage, yourself, and what you believe. Always challenge fear and work diligently to eradicate it.

Sometimes the spirits give us reason to fear them. Many of us will encounter spirits who don't necessarily want the best for us, or who are unable to act on behalf of our good. When this happens, it is because the manner in which they died or the harmful actions they engaged in during their lifetimes are preventing them from making an elevated transition in the spirit world. These *egun* require the help of a medium who can perform the necessary elevation rituals. Once elevated, these difficult ancestors are able to extend good will and energy toward us.

Most of us have more kind and giving ancestors looking out for us than we have troublesome *egun* who look unfavorably upon us or turn away when we need them. Trust that most of your spirits want your life to shimmer with blessings. Believe that they are invested in your healing and spiritual progress, and that they want to see your life's promise fulfilled. They appreciate your attentions to them—the simple and sincere things you do to acknowledge and give to them.

Simple offerings of food, water, and light and calling the spirits by name matter a great deal to them. Elaborate ritual is unnecessary and sometimes inappropriate. It should never be your only means of honoring the spirits. Approaching the ancestors only out of duty and in a prescribed way is ineffective and unwise. Even the information provided in this book is simply a guide, a collection of signposts to help you on your journey rather than a definitive map. Although it is important to observe certain conventions and to worship with integrity, avoid approaching your practice according to a rigid set of dos and don'ts.

The most important thing is to acknowledge and respect your ancestors, to be yourself with them, and to share a little bit of your life with them every day. That is the way to put soul into your daily worship—giving depth to your relationship with your *egun* and laying the groundwork for your relationship with the deities.

Remember, rituals of reverence that are devoid of a genuine and deeply felt intimacy or that are performed with a robotic detachment or in fear will flatten your spiritual connections and parch your ancestral gardens. Opening your heart and accepting the ancestors' love for you will be the center of your ancestral garden. Allow your worship to emerge from that.

Working Daily

One of the ways in which you can become close to the ancestors, especially in the early stages of your practice, is to interact daily with the shrine and by extension with the spirits who gather there. Again, this daily activity doesn't need to be elaborate or time-consuming. Something as simple as sharing your food offers a potent and meaningful gesture, a way of giving back nourishment and life to those who made your existence possible.

Talking to your spirits every day is another powerful medicine to bring your hearts closer. Speak with them about everything: your plans, dreams, struggles, needs, relationships, and work. Share your good news and your gratitude. Say hello in the morning and goodnight when you go to bed.

As my Godmother Obalade says, your ancestors are your roommates and they are always at home, even though it initially may feel as though no one is there or listening. Share the daily mundane details of your life with the spirits and reach out to them in simple ways, just a little each day, and whatever awkwardness you may feel at the beginning will gradually dissolve.

As you become more familiar with the rhythms and needs of your ancestral garden, you will discover the daily devotions that will bring you closer to your people—your unique ways of remembering them, talking to them, and sharing yourself with them.

Honoring Your Commitments

The voice of fear will tell you, "Watch out! Be careful! Keep your word to the spirits, or they'll get mad and begin to punish you." Well, my *egun* have never punished me for anything, not even for the laziness or procrastination that may occasionally keep me from finishing what I've started within the time frame I've committed to. We all do the best we can. We lead hectic lives, and sometimes we don't come through when we say we will. The spirits realize this. I find that as long as I make an honest effort and don't take advantage of their patience, my spirits are very gracious and understanding.

When you don't do something you said you would, rather than feeling guilty and worrying about the wrath of ancestral retribution, let a different set of reasons guide your work with the *egun*. Namely, understand that in any relationship keeping your word fosters trust and openness. Trustworthiness and forthrightness play essential roles in building any relationship, including those between the ancestors and us.

By the same token, if you continually fail to show up when you say you will, although the spirits may not punish you, your lack of consistency will adversely affect your relationship with them. Make the timing of your devotions manageable, so that you don't make your life more stressful by trying to keep to a taxing ritual schedule. Showing up consistently once a month to meditate in front of the shrine will do more to enhance your relationship with your spirits than making a promise to sit daily that you can't realistically keep. In this respect, less can be more. The integrity of your rituals matter more than how frequently you perform them.

Authenticity

There is one thing that is absolutely necessary when dealing with the *egun*. It is authenticity. Being real with our spirits, being able to share with them the truth about what we think and feel, means more than anything else.

If you can't be truthful with your ancestors, you will have a hard time growing soul in your ancestral garden. Without authenticity, you can stay busy all day long doing what you think or have been told are the proper tasks of reverence and never know genuine trust and companionship with your spirits. You can keep the most elaborate *egun* shrine, but if it is filled with inauthentic adornments, it will lack the power to draw and connect your spirits to you. You might as well not have a shrine at all; the effect is the same.

Authenticity—the willingness to be yourself with your spirits—is the most potent fertilizer you can give your ancestral garden.

Listening

The fast-paced culture of compulsive doing that is common in our society does little to support listening, an essential tool for nourishing our spiritual lives. Yet the ancestors and deities continually speak to us, and they have much to teach us if we just listen. They constantly try to show us which steps to take or not to take, to point us toward solutions, to communicate their wisdom, and to bestow upon us their blessings. The ancestors often speak quietly and simply, whispering truths that, if we're not listening closely, we'll miss.

Because we don't know how to listen, we end up missing a lot. Learning to listen to the spirits is a continual process that takes practice. It requires setting aside time to sit still and quietly before the altar—not planning, praying, or making ritual—just meditating and listening. It's about focusing and paying attention, so you can hear the messages coming to you in the serenity of your ancestral garden.

Self-Reflection

Self-reflection is essential to any spiritual practice. When dealing with the spirits, not only is it important to listen to what the *egun* want to share with you, but you also need to pay attention to what you're thinking and feeling about the process of growing and tending your ancestral garden. What are you learning about yourself, your family, and your spirits? What is difficult about your spiritual work, and what flows freely? Are you being real? Are you trying to hide anything, consciously or unconsciously?

Check in with yourself periodically by doing something that brings you closer to your true feelings. Write in your journal. Take solitary walks or exercise. Make collages, poems, or songs about your journey. Find some way to process the winding path of your unfolding.

Is Anybody There?

When we first start keeping an *egun* shrine, we often have a hard time believing that the seeds we planted are actually growing. We might say all the customary prayers, change our water, put out food regularly, go to ceremonies, and talk to our spirits daily. Still in our private moments in front of our altars, we feel a little awkward and strange, admitting only to ourselves that we're not really sure if anyone on the other side is actually listening.

This is natural, especially for grown people who were not raised in families or cultural environments in which the tools and nuances of working with the ancestors were out in the open, accepted, and passed on to the young. If you find yourself doubting the process, don't worry too much about your misgivings. Try not to judge yourself or the process. Just let it be and continue working. Keep coming back. Keep putting out water and candles and flowers and food. Keep reaching out to your spirits, and allow the process to unfold.

Adoptees, people who grew up in foster families or institutions, and others who, for whatever reasons, have been cut off from information about their bloodline families may find it particularly difficult to feel the spirits when they meditate, make ritual, or pray before their altars. If you know little or nothing about your natural ancestors—if the names, places, stories, and pictures of your people have been lost to you—that's okay. What you don't know about your ancestors has no bearing on the fact that they know all about you. Your unfamiliarity with them doesn't discount the fact that from the other side, long before you knew of their existence, they have loved you and done their best to take care of you.

Although I know some Orisa priests will disagree, I don't believe it is necessary for the spirits of our shrines to be directly related to us by blood. I believe it is appropriate to acknowledge the spirits with whom we are connected by heart lines as well as those with whom we share a bloodline. We are family to each other by all sorts of ties. Honor the ancestors who cared for and loved you, whether or not they are your blood relatives. However, do give your blood ancestors prominence. If you want to grace your altar with people not related to you whom you've never known but whose life or work has inspired you, put them on a separate table.

Address your ancestors in whatever way suits you. If you know names, call them by name. If you don't know names, call for them by place: "I pay homage to all of my elevated *egun* who were from . . . the Caribbean, China, Italy, the Middle East, South Carolina, or Mexico." If you know your spirits by language, ask for their blessings that way: "I call upon all of my spirits who were . . . Spanish-, Patois-, Yiddish-, or Fanti-speaking." You can also speak to your ancestors according to their racial, cultural, or ethnic origins: "I give thanks for the love of all my people who were . . . of African descent, or Polynesian, Creole, South American, Russian Jew, Geechee, Choctaw, or Scotch-Irish." You can invoke the blessings of your ancestors by the work they did: "I acknowledge the deep wisdom of all my *egun* who were . . . teachers, farmers, midwives, and healers." When all you can come up with is the knowledge of atrocities they may have suffered, then name those sufferings: "I ask for peace and goodness for all of my ancestors who . . . died in the Middle Passage, in the Holocaust, on the Trail of Tears, or in war."

If you know nothing about your people—not their names, homelands, mother tongues, or work—then with sincerity and confidence that your words will be heard, say simply: "I ask light and blessings for all my elevated ancestors whose names I do not know, including my parents' parents and all their relatives, and their parents and all their relatives, and all those before them." That should cover just about everyone!

Your ancestors have always been aware of you. Keeping an altar will make you more aware of them. Through cultivating this awareness, you will become more consciously involved in the relationship that has always existed between you. Working the garden of your spirits using the tools of your altar opens a channel through which conscious connectedness flows, awakening a heightened intimacy and trust between you and the *egun*.

---

3. *The Concise Oxford Dictionary* (New York: Oxford University Press, 1990), 462.

Chapter 6

Healing and Honoring Your Spiritual Legacy

We all belong to such a far-reaching line of spirits that most of us can't even fathom what that really means. If we're lucky, we may have some sense of those who have preceded us by fifty, a hundred, or even two hundred years. But our lineage stretches back much farther than that, forming a thick chain of ancestral goodness and strength as well as pain and suffering. Imagine, if you can, ancestors whose feet touched the earth, not just a generation or two ago, but centuries ago. Imagine them with you now, their sorrows reflected in yours and their energy cleansing the road in front of you, assisting you in your struggles and whispering ancient wisdom in your ear.

In the West we like to think of ourselves as self-created or as products of our parental upbringing. In reality, we arrive on Earth laden with a combination of blessings and baggage bequeathed to us by all the members of our bloodline, by all our dead relatives, known and unknown. Some of this ancestral knowledge comes to us through our parents and caretakers; some comes from a more distant link.

For example, I learned to love books largely because my mother does; an affection she learned from her mother, a writer and poet, who learned from her father, and so on. I imagine somewhere way back in that part of my lineage, there is a bookmaker or scribe whose life was dedicated to the written word. I have also inherited from my mother a fear of using my gifts to open doors of opportunity, which for years has kept me miserable and barely making ends meet in my work life. This too my mother learned from her mother, who was college-educated but spent her entire adult life living in poverty. My grandmother, in turn, took this in from her Irish mother, who grew up dirt poor and then married into money, but never gave herself permission to enjoy it. Though the money could have allowed them to live more comfortably, she insisted that her little girls wear the same kind of rough woolen stockings she'd grown up wearing.

Sometimes, lineage works on us in subtle but riveting ways. I know my mother cries when she hears Native American chanting because her Indian blood remembers those songs, their purpose and meaning. The first time my hands ripped leaves for an initiation ceremony, they seemed to move of their own accord, as if they already knew the motions, as if one of my ancestors who used leaves for medicine had stepped into my skin. Lineage works from deep within us and makes us who we are and in many ways shapes how we choose to live out our lives.

Clearing Rocky Ground

How do we deal with the rocky ground we sometimes encounter in the ancestral garden? In working with the *egun,* one of our first tasks is to dig down and test the condition of the soil. Is it moist and loamy, or hard and dry? Is it rich with nutrients or lacking in vitality? Has it been depleted or eroded? Does it need to be built up or refortified?

When I first got down to my people's soil all I did was cry, because all I could see were generations of intense family pain and separation. The list of grievances was harsh and long: poverty, loss, ruptured families, incest, disowned and abandoned children, emotional and psychological abuse, shame, addiction, betrayal, and lies. My family story was laden with pain, and it was all I'd ever known. I had no memories of grandmothers or older aunts or other family members who loved and protected me, whom I could count on. My ability to accept the principle that ancestors exist in our world didn't preclude the fact that I could not point to a single one who was a positive presence in my daily life.

The only forebear I'd ever known personally was my maternal grandmother, who was manipulative and narcissistic. During my childhood, our visits to her were sporadic and obligatory, and she and my mother would go through periods of estrangement that sometimes lasted years. I never felt that she liked me, and I didn't like her either. The two or three other ancestors I knew about were people I'd either never known, knew very little about, or associated only with my family's legacy of toxic relationships and severed ties.

I deeply wanted a relationship with my ancestors. I needed to heal the spiritual rift of my lineage and to feel connected to something besides the big empty hole that the ancestors had always meant for me. I knew my involvement with the Orisa tradition could give me this connection with my spirits. I hoped the tradition's rituals for calling, remembering, honoring, and loving the ancestors could transform my life. Yet, I also knew that if I wanted true healing, I could not ignore my feelings of emptiness and loss.

Orisa teaches that your mother's mother is one of your most important ancestors and that she should be given a primary place of reverence on your shrine. So once I'd put my grandmother's picture on the table and started calling her name during my morning prayers, technically I was doing the right thing. I guess I could have left it at that. But it didn't feel like enough, and it seemed like a cover for other unnamed feelings. I decided I wanted to do more than go through the motions and that I couldn't blindly take on a belief system without doing the work needed to internalize the teachings. I began to understand that tending an *egun* shrine, learning to love and feel loved by my spirits, would require looking back into a family story full of wounded spirits. Feeling my ancestors in my daily life would mean feeling the pain of that story.

When I put my hands into the dirt and started pulling things out, trying to find some healthy soil to grow in, I kept coming up with slimy, worm-eaten, smelly old things, twisted pieces of rusted metal, and shards of broken glass left behind by my people before me. I was searching for a clean, soft soil that would make me feel loved and part of something good, capable of nurturing life. But I kept finding generation after generation of unfinished business. It was heavy and painful work—researching my bloodline, asking my mother difficult questions, and learning painful truths about my people. I often had to leave it for a while, to take a break and do something else to replenish my strength so that I could continue my *egun* work. Over the years, I kept digging, using my bare hands, a shovel, or a stick—anything to excavate the junk that interfered with my garden's ability to sustain a robust set of roots.

This cycle of working and digging, finding old pain and grieving, went on for some time. Then one day I realized something inside me had shifted, quietly and from a place deep within. After laboring for a long time in seemingly infertile ground, I discovered not too far below the decimated topsoil an abundance of beautiful black, rich, healthy earth. By pulling out the debris and pain-ridden histories that had choked off my ancestors' beauty, I had unearthed a bountiful mound of sparkling jewels that began to tangibly enrich my life.

Let me say that this excavation is ongoing. Although it can be particularly consuming during the early stages of ancestral gardening, the digging and searching never really stops; the frequency and intensity just lessens. Our family stories are ongoing and too complicated and profound, too full of mysteries and unanswered questions, for most of us to ever finish our ancestral gardening completely. There is always something else to look at, another hard truth to find and free up, so we can keep on healing and developing spiritually. We should not see this as a burden. Instead, we should accept that we may need to dig around in our ancestral grounds from time to time and trust that the old pains we find there will continue to bring healing and beauty.

Accepting the Whole Truth

We may sometimes want to step around the painful aspects of family history by romanticizing or simplifying our view of certain ancestors. For example, as an African-American woman, I cannot remember my black ancestors without looking squarely at the atrocity of slavery. What I would like to remember about my people and slavery is that they survived such tremendous brutality with their spirits intact and that most of my spiritual endowments come straight from them. I would prefer to focus on this side of the truth, to pay witness to the positive aspects of their lineage that have survived, while quietly keeping the other, unpleasant side of that truth buried.

In a sense, it is less painful to see things that way. It is easier to remember my black *egun* in a solely positive light than it is to also look at the injustices they themselves may have committed. I would rather disregard the ways in which my people took the wounds of slavery and turned them upon themselves and each other. I would rather not look at how this caused another kind of damage, one less broad in scope than the institution of slavery, but still damage that continues to reach far beyond the span of their lifetimes into the lives of their descendants today.

Part of me would like to simplify my notion of the white people in my family, with whom I've never had any positive connection. On one hand, I can look at the white side of my lineage and clearly see the painful ways their racism and class privilege have worked like a poison running through a body, devastating our family. But the full and complicated truth is, even if their goodness was not obvious when they were alive, some of my white *egun* do bring me many blessings now that they are dead. I was able to write this book in part because the spirit of my nonconformist Pennsylvania-Dutch-British-Irish grandmother, the one I never had a good word for when she was living, sat down beside me day after day, urging me to stay focused and helping me to be brave enough to say all I needed to say.

The whole story about most families is that they are unavoidably complex and multifaceted. Usually these complexities are caused by painful or unpleasant circumstances in their lives. When we start digging in our gardens and looking back at those lives, we will not be spared the ugly, frightening, and hurtful parts. When we invite the ancestors into our lives, we see the whole truth of their lives and inevitably find the sweet and the sour laced together. The dance of polarities that governs the universe—hot and cold, light and dark, opposing sides forever and intimately bound with one another—takes place in families too. Each family has a sustaining and affirming side as well as a jagged and cutting side. If we look closely, most of us will see at least a few thorny stems growing among the flowers in our ancestral gardens.

How then do we work with the complexities of our personal lineages? What do we do about the weeds that can grow so fast and move so quickly to take over our plots of earth? How do we keep the tangled vines from choking the tender shoots? Well, if we want our gardens to thrive, we must vigilantly remove and control the weeds to prevent them from diverting water and nutrients from the life-sustaining vegetation. This process of approaching the painful areas in our lineage requires time, effort, patience, and a great deal of tenderness for ourselves and eventually for the spirits. It can be back-breaking, hand-blistering, and frustratingly tedious work. But then, we don't do it because it is easy, fun, or painless. We do it because we know we may need to unearth some nastiness in order to free up the joy, peace, and goodness that also grow in our *egun* gardens.

Difficult Feelings

In addition to the unresolved issues the ancestors may leave behind for us to deal with, we also bring seeds of our own weeds to our *egun* gardens. Many of us have resentment and pain connected with certain spirits that weigh us down, impeding our ability to nurture our spirituality.

For some of us, growing a lush ancestral garden is impossible until we figure out what to do with the dead father who drank too much, the violent mother who beat us, or the mean-spirited uncle who neglected and abused us. Just glancing at the web of secrets and lies surrounding certain ancestors can leave us depressed and worn out. Depleted, we may simply parrot our devotions or bypass ancestral work altogether.

Some people try to navigate these hard spaces by saying, "Let it go. It's over. What's in the past should stay in the past." I think that is an incomplete response, because our lives today are inevitably affected by what happened to our families in the past. How we live today impacts how we and those who come after us will live tomorrow. There is no separation between past, present, and future; it is all connected.

Another problem with the what's-done-is-done response to family history is that it encourages the masking of feelings and thus short-circuits our healing. Denying pain just buries pain. When we turn our backs on pain, under the mistaken notion that avoidance will make pain magically disappear, it just shows up someplace else, attached to an even greater crisis, having grown larger, more persistent, and more damaging from our having ignored it.

It might seem easier to operate under the illusion that if we ignore pain, it will go away. But no matter how far or how long we keep painful truths out of sight, we're really just adding them to the mountain of unfinished business that many of us live crouching in the shadow of. In working with my own ancestral garden, I found that in order to have the deep-rooted relationship with my spirits that I so dearly wanted, I needed to tend to the unfinished business they'd left behind and to the unfinished business I had with them.

Before I talk about how to use the *egun* altar to aid in the process of resolving issues with people who are no longer in a body, let me be clear that keeping an *egun* shrine is no substitute for therapy. Working with ritual, prayer, altars, and spirits should not take the place of the kind of in-depth work that requires the support of a skilled and compassionate therapist. When our wounds run so deep that we don't feel up to making the journey alone, we need to find someone who can walk with us at least for a while. In that case, ancestral worship can often help in the therapeutic process. However, whether or not your inner work involves therapy, your altar and the spirits who congregate there can provide a powerful healing force.

In my experience, most spirits elevate to some degree—or at least want to—after leaving their physical bodies. People who have passed over to the invisible realm can often see their relationships with greater insight and compassion than when they were living. Most spirits who visited damage and devastation upon us during their lifetimes want to heal the injuries they've left behind. Even ancestors who committed horribly evil acts in life are capable of healing and elevation in the spirit realm.

When we are in the midst of struggling to heal the traumas inflicted by members of our families who have died, we may feel like casting them out of our ancestral gardens—and we may need to do just that for a while. We may have to temporarily deny them access to the space we make for ancestors both in our homes and in our hearts. Eventually, though, we must at least acknowledge their presence. My elders taught me that we can never disown our *egun*. Our ancestors are our ancestors, period—acts of violation, abuse, and dysfunctional family dynamics notwithstanding. Our irrefutable connection with them cannot be undone. It has been encoded into our blood, whether we like it or not, no matter how deeply they have hurt us or others. That does not necessarily mean we must include them on our altars; it simply means that we must understand and accept the fact that who they were is part of who we are.

I have learned through many years of working with the weeds in my own garden that I hurt as much when I don't call my grandmother's name at the altar as when I do. When I focus on healing the wounds of the painful legacy left to me, I feel more healthy and whole, more me, than when I turn away from the ancestors who have wounded me.

Opening our daily lives to a more resonant and reciprocal ancestral presence requires working to repair and fortify our spiritual legacy. Each of us forms a link in a long ancestral chain, which, for most of us, has been ruptured or somehow damaged. Looking up that chain to find out who is there and how we are connected helps us to recover a cellular soul memory that lives within each of us.

When we exclude certain of our spirits from our ancestral work—even when our resistance to them is wholly justified—the memory chain starts to split apart and the connectedness with our lineage weakens. I am not saying that we should always include these ancestors in our prayers or at our shrines. However, our resistance to these unwelcome spirits should serve as a reminder of where we still need to work on healing our injuries. We should continue to work with the intent and hope of one day mending ourselves enough so that we are able and willing to include those spirits on our altars. With that gesture we begin to release them, which in turn releases us from the pain they have caused. That process may take months, years, or decades. The key is not to ride roughshod over your feelings. Real healing comes from carefully investigating and tending to our wounds.

Be Honest

I am well aware that this wound-tending and peacemaking is frequently easier said than done. It took more than ten years of diligent work for me to include one of my great-grandfathers on my ancestral table. He was an upstanding white man who disowned my mother, his only grandchild, because she was, as he said, a "nigger." Even though I knew all along that excluding him from my *mojuba* is not what I should have done, I needed to be true to my process. I could not put him on my shrine until my heart told me to, until I had worked out some of my anger toward him, and until I'd given his spirit ritual elevation. Only then was it safe for me to attempt to get closer to him.

Now that he is on my altar, he has shown me his sorrow and his desire for reconciliation. Even so, I continue to wade through my complicated and difficult feelings. Putting him on the altar does not mean that there is no more work to be done, that I have fully forgiven him, or that the gash his rejection caused our family has healed over. It merely says that together we can now take the next small steps toward mending this broken part of the family story we share.

In my work with the *egun*, they continue to teach me that often the same ancestors who hurt us during their lives are now in the spiritual realm, seeking atonement for having caused that pain. These spirits need to heal from their transgressions as much as we need to heal from what they've done to us. Supporting our healing gives them a way to move toward their own redemption. We have to be willing to involve them in the healing process.

To take on this joint effort, we must first tell the truth about how we feel. That often means opening ourselves to wrenching emotions over messy family dynamics, relationships, and histories. I have seen many people shy away from the deeper layers of *egun* work because they have too many painful and unresolved feelings around deceased family members who have hurt them. They avoid the pain, either because they don't want to get past it or don't feel they can. The point is not to get over it, but to embrace those feelings and use them as a way to move into a more meaningful relationship with the ancestors. The key is to tell the truth, take your time, and not skip any steps. Be true to your experience, be gentle with yourself, and be willing to accept whatever your relationship with your *egun* brings.

Ritualize the Process

When feeling my way through some of the painful parts of my ancestral story, I often used a sort of talking-prayer ritual. I start by bringing some freshly brewed coffee to my spirits and telling them I need to purge some old feelings that are getting in the way of my feeling connected to them. Then I sit down and let my feelings come out in whatever way they need to.

These feelings and the words that carry them are not pretty. They emerge in raised voices, burning with accusation, rage, or grief, peppered with prayers for healing. I don't worry about whether they're appropriate or well-organized. They may not even be what others would call respectful. But they are true. They are honest. Time after time they have lit the way to a more soulful connection with my spirits, guiding me like trusted scouts into the luminescent mines containing the spiritual wealth of my lineage.

If you take a similar walk-through-fire approach, don't try to process too much internally or with anyone else immediately afterward. Trust that your raw truthfulness will become its own prayer. You don't have to do anything more to further the process. Your honesty will benefit your relationship with your ancestors probably in subtle ways that you won't even notice at first.

This kind of prayer as grieving can deplete you, so it is important to nurture yourself afterward. Rest. Eat a good, healthy dinner that doesn't require a lot of energy to prepare. Soak in a tub of warm, fragrant water or replenish yourself with non-strenuous activities that make you feel cared for. Stay away from television, drugs, alcohol, gregarious talk, and loud music. When you go to sleep, place a glass of water near the head of your bed and pour it out the next morning. Place fresh water on your altar and light a new white candle. Put a small bowl of honey on the shrine and spend a few moments in front of your spirits before starting your day.

Also, before engaging in this type of inner work, carefully consider whether the situation and emotions you're dealing with warrant the assistance of a professional therapist. If that is the case, don't do this work alone—make sure you have the support you need.

The process of healing your lineage wound is unique to each practitioner. I encourage you to allow your process to unfold for you in the way it wants to. Use my way only as guide to finding your own. Be yourself. Embrace your feelings. Tell the truth. If you are angry, be angry. If you were hurt, say so. If you need to cry or yell, do it. Mourn what was taken from you and grieve for what you never had. Give voice to your feelings about bad things that happened in the past and have been festering inside you. Then you can begin breaking down the walls that have kept you from sharing a full heart with your spirits.

When we have the courage to stand before the *egun* shrine and speak to our spirits about familial pain and their part in perpetuating it, something soulfully nourishing and reciprocal takes place. Given the chance to witness our suffering and knowing they helped create it, the ancestors invariably show up with regret, humility, and compassion. They want us to heal from the hurt they handed down to us. Their elevation and health on the other side may even require it. Our spirits play an invaluable role in lightening our burden, and they are eager to claim it.

One of the lessons we learn from this work is that there are broad forces in the world that sometimes negatively influence the actions of our *egun*. Powerful societal and institutional systems as well as trans-generational familial patterns have often affected the choices made by our ancestors, including those who now cause us to suffer. Our ancestors left us the pain they inherited from their *egun*, who in turn were hurt by people and events that came before them, and so on.

This perspective softens my heart a little, allowing me to see that even my great-grandfather, privileged as he was by his whiteness and wealth, also suffered from the lie of racial superiority he so fiercely clung to. His racism took from him the joys of grandfatherhood. He died a sick and embittered man, with none of his children near him. Now, three generations later, I know that his spirit is humbled by the irony that his only living descendants are not white. Not a single white person is left from his bloodline to hold his memory—just me, the amber-skinned, full-lipped daughter of his daughter's "niggerchild."

Ancestral Blessing

Though we need to work through the plots of injury and suffering if we are to grow roots of connectedness and trust with the *egun*, none of us inherit ancestral sorrow alone. Just as we each walk with a piece of our ancestors' pain, we also carry some of their blessings and magic.[4]

Mixed in with everything that hurts about where I come from is the other side of that truth. For every piece of pain my ancestors have given me, they have put in my hands something beautiful—a gift, an ability, a strength, a sensitivity. Everything I do that makes me happy and creates goodness in the world is connected in some fundamental way to my lineage. For all my people knew about abuse and suffering, they also knew about making medicine, beauty, prayer, and healing. They knew about art and music, living with passion, and staying close to the land.

Each of us is the beneficiary of an ancient ancestral insight, a knowing, that is unique to our heritage. Those blessings have the power to unleash a tremendous force that can right what is out of balance in our lives and can restore the mind, body, heart, and spirit.

Your *egun*'s special gifts may be working with leaves, sound, hot rocks, or sticks. Perhaps your people knew the secrets of the mountain or salt water. Maybe they worked with weaving and sewing or were masters of drum medicine. Maybe you have an ancestor who can help you learn divination, woodworking, midwifery, or how to play the piano. You may have a spirit who can teach you about how to fix things or succeed in business.

Whatever you do or want to do, your ancestors are waiting to teach you the uses and powers of their gifts. Ask your *egun* to reveal to you the spiritual riches and tools of your lineage, and to teach you how to use them for wellness and healing. Let them show you how to unlock the magic that gave strength to their prayers and nurtured goodness in their lives. It will do the same for you.

Building relationships with my ancestors has opened up my life in extraordinarily profound and healing ways. Today I tend the grounds of a much different ancestral garden than the one I first grappled with. That early wrestling with rocky soil, with feelings of separation and awkwardness, have quietly and gradually given way to a garden bursting year-round with vibrant color, sweet fragrance, and succulent fruit. By getting to know the spirits of my lineage, my life has been transformed. You can do the same with your life.

If you are on the path of Orisa, you already know that the ancestors lead us to most essential parts of our tradition. If you are just beginning to walk this road, you will soon develop this understanding. I offer you these little reminders to carry with you as you go:

- Start simple.
- Move slowly but steadily.
- Be yourself.
- Let your heart lead.
- Be willing to look into your lineage pain.
- Apprentice yourself to your ancestral wisdom.

Pursue this work with passion and commitment, and you will find, rising up out of your own fertile ground, the soul of your people with all its fullness and blessing.

---

4. Iyalorisha Obalade, oral instruction.

PART THREE

ONA RE'O,
THE ROAD OF BLESSING

People come to Orisa with different needs. Many are content to approach our tradition as outsiders, for example, as intellectuals who study our rituals and teachings. Others are peripheral participants, involved in the life of the community but only from the edge, attending public ceremonies on occasion, and consulting a diviner when needed. They consider themselves believers but do not fully embrace the tradition. For some people, approaching the Orisa tradition this way is sufficient and consistent with their highest good. Not everyone needs to move beyond those parameters, or should do so. The soul of Orisa, however, cannot be found in books or informal worship; this requires a formal commitment to daily practice and initiation.

Initiation is based on the belief that physical existence is but one facet of life and that it exists alongside a spiritual reality. Seers are people whose expanded consciousness enables them to cross the threshold between the material realm and the spiritual realm. Keeping one foot in each reality, they gather information in the otherworld and bring it back for others to learn from in the physical world.

Initiation is a means of preparing for this work, expanding a person's ability to perceive, understand, engage, and make positive use of spirit forces. This expansion requires a period of total immersion and integration into the spiritual realm. Therefore, initiation always involves some form of separation from one's usual life. Suspending regular habits, the novice leaves behind the familiar and enters into sacred space, which is prepared by the elders. These elders guide and support the student through rituals of transformation. After the initiate surrenders to the spirit forces, she returns from initiation reborn.

In Yoruba tradition, initiation brings forth the most profound understanding of the gods and our relationship with them. It introduces us to their world and invites their sacred energies into our daily lives to reshape and renew us from the inside out.

Chapter 7

Choosing Your Path to God

According to our elders, the most transformational path to knowledge of the divine mysteries is available only to those who make the commitment to initiation. Yet many of us walk into initiation naively, chasing the glitter but lacking basic information. We may secretly hope that initiation will yield some miraculous resolution to a challenging or painful part of our lives. However, soon we realize we've been caught ill-prepared. We come face to face with our fantasy or misunderstanding about what we expected initiation to bring, and we are stunned by what we find once it is over. Yes, the experience changes us and the world we live in, often in subtle ways we can barely discern. But in typical *both/and* Yoruba fashion, we find we still have issues to deal with. The process of initiation doesn't make our troubles and sorrows suddenly go away; it just gives us another set of tools for working on them.

The paradox is that initiation can actually answer many of our unconscious desires. Many people find that after initiation their hearts mend, their prosperity increases, their self-love deepens, and their stability grows. Despite the dramatic shifts and sudden healing that initiation can bring,

Orisa is a path of transformation, not salvation. Though the ancestors and Orisa always support us, there are no rescue teams swooping in to save the day, and there are no quick fixes. On this path, we don't become liberated from difficulty. Our religion is simply a catalyst for change, providing opportunities for growth and healing, and giving us divine guidance in making choices that will either facilitate or impede our journeys. We matters most is our commitment to honor our soul's desire to fulfill its original covenant, and our willingness to ask ourselves this question: am I on the path my soul chose for me?

Religion and Spirituality

In order to understand what it means to cross the threshold of initiation to formal practice, we must first understand religion and spirituality, how they differ from and yet compliment one another. Religion is the outer shell, the external manifestation of spirituality. It concerns itself with form, hierarchy, and ritual; with the continuity of teachings; and with maintaining the rules that ensure continuity. Religion teaches us important things, such as the attributes of the gods, how to shave the head of the novice, and how to pray someone through the stages of spiritual rebirth.

Yoruba religion usually involves external, often communal actions—learning, using, and passing on our ceremonies, rituals, prayers, and divination tools. We learn these formal practices from our teachers, the elders, whose instruction provides us with a foundation and a framework for worship.

Spirituality is a little different, its focus more internal. Whereas religion is the study of teachings and ritual, spirituality is a highly personal journey into the recesses of meaning and mystery hidden beneath the skin of any tradition. Spirituality focuses less on how and why we make ritual and less on public displays of knowledge and protocol, and more on our intention and integrity when performing the ritual. Religion tends to be more structured, expressed outwardly through standards of conduct and worship that are usually defined (and policed) by the priesthood. Spirituality, on the other hand, is more open-ended, personal, and private, with the manner of practice shaped by the individual's unique journey and needs.

At the core of spirituality is a desire for deep relationship and oneness with God. Whether you call God by the name Olodumare, Jesus, Allah, or the Great Spirit, what matters spiritually is how deeply you want to expand your awareness of God as ever present. The issue then becomes how fully you open your life to your religious principles and how committed you are to demonstrating those principles in your daily life. Spirituality is the essence, the true purpose, and the highest function of religion.

Yet spirituality and religion often travel divergent paths. You may be religious and not at all spiritual; you can live a spiritual life with no ties to religion; or you can integrate your religious practice with your spirituality. Religion without spirituality frequently ends up separating people. One group that worships one way sets itself apart from another that worships another way. Each side gets caught up in the differences in their ideology of God and takes opposing positions of what's right and what's wrong, forgetting the common ground we all stand on.

A spiritual approach to religion seeks to bypass those kinds of unproductive discussions, acknowledging that a fully awakened connection with God requires the same basic effort from all of us, regardless of the manner in which we cultivate that relationship. The name or nature of our chosen religion doesn't matter—we all turn to worship for the same reasons and to do the same types of work. We all have work to do on ourselves—to learn more about love, compassion, and humility, the universal spiritual directives that underlie all religions.

In the end it is simpler than many of us think. More important than the specifics of our ideology and rituals are the integrity and authenticity of our worship, our willingness to learn, and our ability to integrate God into our daily lives. When we strive to become living vessels for the best teachings of our various religions, the unique beauty of our respective traditions flows more freely through our thoughts, feelings, words, and deeds. The difference in the way we talk to God is not as significant as the imprint left behind by the choices we make in the name of our relationship with God.

A religion is made great not by the structure it provides its people, but by how deeply that structure nourishes the individual soul's need for spiritual attunement and growth.

Conversely, a person's spiritual nature often flows more freely when it has the structure and history of a religious tradition to support it.

Unfortunately, in many religious circles, including Yoruba-centered ones, spirituality is often overlooked or undervalued. In part that is because finding and navigating a personal spiritual path is usually more challenging than adhering to the established practices of a given religion. For example, though it may take years of hard work to learn how to interpret the oracle and how to perform an initiation, these processes are fairly clear-cut. Most of us can master the mechanics of religious practices through instruction from our elders, observation, and repeating the rituals and prayers over time.

A spiritual life, however, typically requires us to visit the wild lands of our interior landscape. For most of us, this deeper self is full of mystery and challenging emotions, memories, and needs. Learning about the self is rarely a clearly marked and linear path. The quality of our personal spiritual paths is reflected not in how well we perform certain practices, but in our ability to grapple with such difficult questions as: *Am I living an authentic life? Do I really love myself? Am I compassionate enough, humble enough? How am I treating people, especially those with less power or position than me? Am I paying attention? Where do I need to grow, to listen, and to understand?*

Spirituality challenges us to learn about ourselves as we simultaneously learn about our religion. It requires us to open our hearts as we increase our knowledge, to honor God within our souls as well as through our actions. Part of what makes life with Orisa so rewarding is the seamless manner in which our tradition connects religion and spirituality, allowing room for both our religious and spiritual natures. The Yoruba religion offers up a multitude of opportunities for spiritual lessons about self-knowledge and about our connectedness with God. Focusing on our spiritual development keeps us working on ourselves. As we heal old wounds and deepen our spirituality, we gradually extend this expanded self to Orisa. As we become healed and more connected to God, we are better equipped to help others. This enhances our religious activity, making us more constructive contributors to both our religious communities and the world community.

At this juncture—where religion and spirituality meet to nourish and support each other—we find the soul of Yoruba tradition. When we commit ourselves to learning everything we can from our religious elders and to using daily life as a spiritual teacher, our spiritual-religious work carries us beyond the mere concept of breathing with God. We get closer to the possibility of becoming a living demonstration of it. When we are willing to become more conscious of self, to work from the premise that God is all there is, and to integrate religious practice with spiritual sensibility, we find the sacred marrow at the core of Orisa.

Clear Purpose, Pure Intention

In Orisa, a commitment to formal practice is always guided by our religious elders (or godparents) and is usually supported by our religious communities. But this commitment begins with and depends upon the initiate's personal intentions and choices. Many of us make important life choices unconsciously without taking the time and effort to look closely at where those choices are likely to take us, where we're going, the road we're likely to travel to get there, and what we may encounter along the way. Stepping on to the Orisa path with eyes half-closed can get us into big trouble. When we enter initiation without awareness, naive to the complex way initiation works on our lives, it can have serious repercussions, some of which can never be undone. It is crucial to know what led you to this important juncture in your journey and whether initiation is really the road you want to travel.

Some of us choose initiation after attending public ceremonies and witnessing the love with which the gods, while in possession of their priest-mediums, tend to the devoted—cleansing, assisting, and offering them counsel. Just one such encounter with the Orisa's kindness can cause tremendous shifts within us, pulling us toward the deities and their teachings. Sometimes we come to formal practice because we know intuitively or have been told through divination that a more committed involvement will restore wholeness to our lives.

Often, we pursue initiation out of some sort of need. We might feel lost or fragmented and long for a connection with something larger, wiser, and more loving to restore order and balance to our lives. It is entirely appropriate to come to the Orisa in need or seeking fulfillment. That's what they're for, to help us lead more satisfying, soulful lives. The danger comes when our neediness and confusion overwhelm us, clouding our ability to see what we're getting involved with. We may secretly or openly hope that initiation will help us bounce back from a breakup, improve our finances, or bring us status and power. We may seek initiation to fill an emotional void, or because our partner is initiated and we don't want to feel left out. Sometimes we try to replace a troubled biological family with an idealized religious one. Whatever the underlying reasons that lead us to the door of initiation, we must name them and be honest with ourselves about what they are, so we can face the Orisa and our spiritual work with integrity. If we are not tuned in to our conscious and unconscious desires for initiation, we may find more pain and fewer answers than we bargained for.

Even those whose intention is simply to come closer to God often don't realize that in order for that to happen, they will first need to shed any protective coverings around their lives. This disrobing process can be unsettling if you are unaware that you've enclosed yourself in spiritual armor or if you are unprepared for what you find underneath it.

When we are not wholly conscious of our spiritual needs, we cannot articulate them or determine whether and how initiation might help us meet them. Before committing to formal practice, initiates should have a clear idea of what they expect to give and get from Orisa. If they have any questions or are confused, they should seek the counsel of an elder, someone wiser who might just say, "You know what? If what you're looking for is an escape route or a smooth road, you might want to rethink this." As every person who has become a priest of Orisa knows, this is a path of immeasurable beauty and never-ending hard work.

Seduced by the Glitter

Many of us want to see God and God's power on the big screen. We want religion to give us instantaneous and radical change, excitement, and fireworks. We want our spiritual practice to thrill and amaze us, to feed our hunger for drama and intensity. Many elements of Orisa do, in fact, fulfill those desires. Our celebrations and rituals can indeed be intense experiences filled with beauty and excitement.

Sometimes *aleyos*, or non-initiates, become enamored of the tradition's outward magnificence. They see the joy the priesthood brings to the *olorisha* and assume it comes from the radiance of our tradition's external practices—and it does, but only in part. Many priests do love making altars for the Orisa, dancing and singing at ceremonies, and participating in our potent rituals. Outward expression is a vital outlet for our devotion and reverence. But priests also know that the real source of our joy is something internal, enhanced by, but not born of, the magnificence of our rituals.

The real thrill and gifts of the tradition cannot be found in any public ceremony or initiation rite. Priests of Orisa know that only when we go beyond the splendor of altar-making, of seeing Orisa in possession, and of receiving messages from the gods do we encounter the true wonder of our tradition. We know we find the true blessing of our faith by descending into the nitty-gritty of our lives and gradually surrendering all to God. We also know the tremendous work involved in such deep layers of worship.

It is understandable how non-initiates might become enchanted by the brilliance of Orisa's cloak and might mistakenly assume their own blessings will derive from that outer surface. But they need to know that Orisa priests and priestesses do not always show the scars we've acquired from toiling in the fields of our inner landscapes. *Aleyos* must understand that it has taken years of struggle for us to reshape our lives so we can be closer to God, to really know and be known by Orisa.

The deities have a remedy for the syndrome of the starstruck *aleyo*. He is Elegua, the Orisa who guards the threshold and who in his trickster mode seduces the unsuspecting with the magic and ceremony of Yoruba tradition. Letting us fall on our faces is one way Elegua teaches us to choose more consciously. Those among us in need of this lesson will find Elegua—ruler of the feet—perched mischievously between our toes, saying, "Careful now. Watch where you walk. You think that's what this is all about? Well, I've got something for you." Then he proceeds to set us up to follow the path of enchantment until we encounter the deeper lessons brought by Orisa and the illusion is shattered. Of course, we each hold the power to decide whether to embark upon that path and to then learn from that choice.

If you are a non-initiate who's been carried along by the attractiveness of the tradition, when your illusion breaks down—as it inevitably will—your soul will have an opportunity to open to a more complex and transformative view of Orisa, provided you are willing. At that point, you can begin to allow the gods into your life on a more intimate basis, enabling them to show you themselves on the real big screen. You can watch the true story unfold—quietly, slowly, and without fanfare—as the Orisa fill all the big and small places of your life with their luminous love. Then you, like the *olorishas,* will know the true meaning of enchantment.

Be Informed

Many Orisa practitioners, regardless of the path that carries them there, come to formal practice with too little information. We seek spiritual renewal, but we're not really clear what that entails. Distracted by our needs, we often neglect to find out what the tradition is really about. Dazzled by Orisa's accouterments—the altars and ceremonies, the energy and magic, the priests in possession, the divine messages from the gods and the ancestors—we fail to see their true purpose.

We jump into initiation lacking this critical insight, because we don't realize we need it, or we don't really want to know. Too often we ask the wrong questions of our elders or they fail to give us the information we need to make informed choices. We then move forward with a skewed notion of what rebirth requires and brings us. The one thing we must understand before asking Orisa to show us the way to our destiny is this: rebirth and renewal come with a price.

Anyone who is considering making a commitment to Orisa should first spend some time watching an old home being renovated. It's easy to see that the first step of any renovation is getting rid of all the old, worn-out stuff. As you watch those old walls come down, envision your inner walls being knocked away. Close your eyes and feel the two-by-fours cracking apart within you. Watch as dirty window-panes shatter—windows through which you might have once viewed the world clearly. Imagine what it might feel like to be the sagging, worn carpet being ripped up from an old stairway, exposing the stairs that have been hidden beneath it for years. Imagine an intricate process of replacing plumbing and electrical systems, the focused concentration required to find and repair broken channels and circuitry. Observe as creaking floorboards are stripped bare, sanded, oiled, and buffed to their original smoothness and shine. Imagine an ancient house moaning as it is broken down, shored up, and hammered back together from the foundation up. Watch as workers toil, removing the house's battered and broken parts, in order to restore its strength and beauty. See them sweat, grow tired, rest, eat, and return to work day after day. Notice the concentration, exertion, skill, and care they devote to their jobs. Understand their frustration and determination as they work to revive the house from years of abuse and neglect. Feel their jubilation along with their calluses and aching backs as they see it slowly rise before them, restored, reborn.

Before you begin the first stage of initiation, make sure you understand what you're getting into. Decide whether you are willing to do the hard inner work that goes into restoring your spiritual home. Ask whether you are prepared to turn yourself over to the master builders of the human spirit, the Orisa, as they tear you down and build you back up again.

Chapter 8

Stepping onto the Path

Initiation into the Orisa tradition brings the initiate powerful lessons about a dynamic force that can be dangerous if not used properly and carefully. This force, which we all possess and use daily whether we realize it or not, is the combined energy of choice and change. Though essentially neutral, this force is extremely potent because it takes on whatever nature or shape we give it. The need to fully understand the power of our capacity to choose is one of Orisa's essential lessons.

Orisa asks us to be accountable for our choices on many levels. First and central is our ability to continually choose and rechoose a path that carries us toward our own destiny. The Yoruba pantheon recognizes numerous gods and goddesses, each of whom performs vital functions on Earth and within our lives. The deities do influence our choices, as do the ancestors, our elders, and our communities. Ultimately, however, we alone make our choices, and we alone are responsible for the consequences of our choices.

Of the many choices a Yoruba initiate makes, the most important by far is choosing her or his personal deity, or *ori*.

The Wise and Sacred Head

The Yoruba word *ori* means head. In Orisa, head is understood as having two primary components: *ori ode*, the outer head, and *ori inu*, the inner head. *Ori ode* is the physical head—brain, skull, and flesh—and is revered as the container for the inner head. *Ori inu* holds one's inherent nature: the core self or soul we are each born with, which seeks to unfold its highest potential during our lives.

Both the inner and outer *ori* receive a great deal of attention in Orisa rituals, for without the strong alignment of our inner and outer heads, we are unable to make the best use of the rest of what the gods have to offer. In this sense, knowing God intimately is contingent upon how deeply connected we are to ourselves.

Aligning Your Head

Yoruba teachings say that before reincarnating into a body, each soul kneels before the Creator in Orun (heaven) and chooses its own *ori* as well as the fundamental destiny for that head. We each choose our essential self—our parents, basic temperament, great loves, major life traumas, soul wounds, and lessons. We choose our gifts, talents, and the life work that will be our highest calling and our most vital contribution to others. We choose the day of our birth and the day of our death. This is all written in bold ink, and for the most part, these choices are firm and unchanging. Though we cannot die after the date *ori* has chosen for us, we can choose unwise life choices that cause us to die before our rightful time.

I know I chose my mother and my father (may he rest in peace) as well as everything that being a part of them has brought me, good and bad. I recognize that before coming to Earth I made an agreement with Olodumare to be loud and sensitive, an artist and a spiritualist, a mother and my brothers' sister, part dragon and part water lily.

While I chose the innermost heart of my destiny in that pre-birth conversation with Olodumare, what I could only partially choose at that time is the way that destiny would unfold in the physical realm. Since my arrival on Earth, I have been creating my path step by step as I move though life. My *ori* gave me the blueprint of the destiny I asked for. Whether I create the life contained in that blueprint is another matter altogether.

In the Yoruba mind, destiny is both predetermined and flexible. We each choose our destiny before conception, but how we respond to life once we get here can change that destiny, either positively or negatively. Our progress in life is largely determined by how well we are aligned with the *ori* we chose at Olodumare's feet. But by the time we're ready to embark upon a spiritual path, many of us have become disconnected from our *ori* by allowing our externally influenced outer heads to overrule our inherently spiritual internal heads. For that reason, a critical first step and the ongoing process in any initiation journey is to rediscover and embrace our sacred head and its divine destiny.

Good Head and Bad Head

From a Yoruba perspective, the parameters shaping our responses to life are drawn by whether we select *ori're*, good head, or *ori'bi*, bad head.[1] Again, this is a choice we make before we are born. For Orisa devotees, this pre-birth choice is disclosed to us through divination. People who measure the goodness of their life by material success or by any other physical outcome usually have a superficial take on what makes a head good or bad. The outward conditions of your life can have little to do with whether you walk with *ori're* or *ori'bi*. The wealthy people haven't necessarily chosen good heads and the poor people bad ones, for example. Wealthy people can die without having fulfilled their life purposes just as less privileged people can live great and soulfully satisfying lives. What we choose before birth is a range of potential that spans the arc of the destinies we've chosen.

One of my elders, an *iyalorisha* named Brandy Canty-Ola Efun, has this wonderful saying, "If you're a pint, be a pint. If you're a quart, be a quart." In other words, quarts are not necessarily better than pints, though they may be taller and have more volume. Pints and quarts should not hunger after each other's destinies, but should accept their own characteristics without trying to be alike or better than each other. Pints should figure out what it really means to be a pint; quarts should pursue the total experience of being a quart. They should then make it their mission to become the most magnificent pintly pints or quartly quarts they possibly can.

We should honor our individuality and differences. We should understand that, within our chosen destinies no matter how big or small they may seem, personal excellence and self-realization are always within reach, even though we may have to stretch a ways to get there.

What makes a good head is not its current situation or even its potential, but its capacity to use life's blessings and hardships as tools for learning and as fuel for progress. A good head is more likely to fulfill its destiny, because it can transform the effects of negative influences into something positive, allowing that life to move forward. A bad head may choose a wonderful destiny, but its inability to make good choices may obstruct movement toward that destiny. *Ori'bi* is the most insidious form of self-sabotage.

The two antidotes for a bad head are ritual cleansing and character-building. A person with *ori'bi* will need to offer her head some medicine for realignment and balance on a regular basis. In Yoruba tradition, these remedies include ritual applications of cool water, coconut, white clay, cocoa butter, cotton, fruit, fish, white cloth, and softly spoken prayer. She also will need to work on becoming a person of good and humble character. She should not treat people unkindly, misuse her authority, or take advantage of others. These acts will undermine her humility and also create unnecessary drama in her life. Drama and self-created chaos will distract her from claiming her life's highest purpose, hard enough to achieve given her bad head. With time and perseverance, ritual cleansing and good character will break down the obstruction of bad headedness that derailed her pursuit of her rightful destiny.

Just like a bad head, a good head also requires humility in order to fulfill its potential. A good head that does not maintain its commitment to humility can gradually veer off the path and collide into obstacles. In that respect, both good head and bad head are somewhat fluid entities, which can be either enhanced by the person's integrity or diminished by his or her lack of integrity.

I don't think anyone has an exclusively bad or good head. Though there always is a primary influence, we all probably have some of each. Generally speaking, mine is a good head—but I certainly have my bad-head days, weeks, and months. Looking back, I'm sure there've been a few bad-head years as well. The important question is which type of head dominates. If the flow of our lives is moving us closer to full and pure expression of our truest self, chances are we have more good head than bad head. As long as we remain committed to cultivating our own good character, we will likely recover and fulfill our chosen destinies.

Regardless of whether we've chosen an essentially good or bad head, I believe the destinies of all people contain the same basic and good ingredients: We all come to Earth having chosen our right to love, purpose, and self-respect. Some of us may also have chosen a set of conditions that make it much harder for us to draw from our ori's legacy to create self-actualized and fulfilling lives. But even under dire circumstances, whether we chose a good head or a bad head, we all have the potential to achieve our destinies.

Of course, the tricky part about working with the power of choice is that we must first know such a power exists and that we can access and channel it. The way we learn about this power is from the people around us. If from an early age our most prominent teachers have been abuse, poverty, oppression, violence, addiction, loss, and terror, we're likely to learn very little about our power to choose. These conditions and the messages they produce can severely damage and disable us. However, it takes only one person who is invested in our progress and who offers an empowering message to steer us in a more positive direction. Unfortunately, if we've been too badly damaged, if no one has ever shown us that even the tightest spaces allow room for choosing, then the goodness an *ori* has chosen for itself can be wasted and essentially undone.

Nonetheless, each person's *ori* is like a lighthouse beacon; it is the part of us that is always in deep communion with God. *Ori* never forgets its true purpose, even if we and others may. Its persistent intention is to move us toward our respective destinies, no matter what the outer conditions of our lives may look like.

Ori can overcome tremendous obstacles in its quest to give us the lives we came here for. It can draw us to the one person who will be instrumental in helping us turn our lives around. *Ori* can pull us out of devastating life circumstances or give us the strength to find a way out when we see no way. The light of *ori* remains constant and strong. What may dim it is our ability to see well in the darkness that at times covers our lives. This can cause us to lower our sights, expecting less of others and ourselves, giving less to life, and receiving less in return.

Yoruba elders teach that our *ori* is the essential soul-self and guardian of one's most sacred purpose, potential, and creative endowments. *Ori* has sacred knowledge of what we came here to do, teach, and give. But because we all make a stop at the tree of forgetfulness en route to the earthly plane, the challenges arise after we choose our destinies. Upon arriving on Earth, we all forget what we have chosen and agreed to embody. Life then becomes a process of remembering our original, pre-earthly agreements.

Life is the journey of realigning ourselves with *ori* and its mission, an arduous challenge that some meet more readily, fully, and quickly than others. A central purpose of initiation, especially the priesthood rite, is to realign initiates with their *ori*. Through ceremony and prayer, initiation touches each person's most essential and God-connected nature, calling it out and giving it the ability to flow with greater ease and less obstruction through one's life. When *ori* is in flow, so are we—living purposeful, meaningful, and self-actualizing lives. When life isn't working well for us, it is usually because we are living in ways that run contrary to the agreements we made with the Creator. Initiation is a ritual adjustment of our life position in relation to our head. It gives us an opportunity for rebirth into our most authentic and God-centered selves.

Finding Your Head Orisa

Every *ori* needs help staying in balance in order to fulfill its destiny. When we choose our head prior to our descent to Earth, we also choose the deity whose *ashe* is most healing and balancing for that head.

I sometimes imagine my pre-earthly meeting with the Creator, when I chose my head, and the Orisa who would rule it.

After I have chosen my destiny, Olodumare calls together the deities. As they sit assembled side by side before me, Olodumare tells me I will be accompanied on my journey into life by all of the Orisa. Like a divinely sanctioned support team, their purpose is to love me unconditionally. They will help me remember and live out all the Creator and I have just discussed, which upon leaving for Earth I will soon forget.

Olodumare then asks: "Which Orisa will you choose as your special guide? Whose temperament aligns most closely with your truest nature? Whose ashe will help you learn your most important lessons? Whose energies will best assist you in uncovering your own essence?"

I select Yemaya, although I have to think about it for a minute, because a few of the other Orisa catch my eye. I feel a strong pull toward Oshun, adorned in brass beads and shimmering gold cloth, her fragrant amber-scented breath sweetening the air. I also feel drawn to Obatala, a tall, quiet old man who exudes peaceful calm. Everything about him is simple, clean, and tender.

Olodumare reminds me that only one deity can fill the position of my ruling or head Orisa. Besides, even though Obatala and Oshun attract me, when I look across the room at that wide-hipped, pregnant-bellied woman with giant seaweed hair, I know I belong with her. Draped in varying shades of turquoise and azure, her blue-black indigo skin salty wet and dripping with pearls, I have no doubt: she is the one who fits me most completely. The moment her sparkling blue eyes meet mine, Olodumare calls her name: "Yemaya!" She bows her head and steps forward. Wrapping her thick, shell-laden arms around me, she speaks quietly into my ear, telling me she'll be waiting for me and that I should look for her once I get to Earth.

Because of my strong feelings for Oshun, the Creator asks her to look after me until Yemaya and I can meet again. Olodumare tells me: "In exchange for the tender care Oshun will give you, once you find Yemaya and are initiated into deep relationship with her, whatever you do for her, remember to do also for Oshun, who will always have a special place in your heart and in your home."

Then Obatala asks if he may serve as Yemaya's second set of hands and eyes. Olodumare gives him the job of co-parent, telling me that although Yemaya will claim my head, Obatala and I will be very close, his words my greatest teachers, his heart my most important guide.

As the scene begins to fade, in that instant just before my soul crystallizes into cell, flesh, and bone, I forget everything. As the last thread of memory rushes out of me,

Yemaya opens her mouth full of water and spits a tiny bead of turquoise salt onto my tongue. She says, "I love you. Use this to remember, it will guide you home to me."

Formal practice, then, is about making the return journey to the Orisa you asked for at the moment you knelt in Olodumare's innermost chamber. It provides an opportunity to seek reunion with the deity who stepped forward to embrace you when Olodumare asked your soul to speak its choices. Rejoining with your head Orisa will require your concerted effort, and ultimately it is your choice if and how you do it.

Life, from that first choice of head and Orisa, is all about choosing. The same is true of our formal spiritual-religious practice. From the moment we first cast our eyes toward the tradition, we are faced with profound lessons about the immense and often hidden power of choice.

Choosing Your Godparent

Yoruba culture is deeply reverent toward the elders, who are your gateway into the tradition. In the Yoruba view, age makes us wiser because with the passage of time we can learn important lessons about life cycles and change. Presumably, old people were once young people who learned of life from the elders around them. They then set out to apply those lessons, meeting all sorts of challenges and success in the process. The longer we live, the more change we witness and overcome. The more graceful we become at drawing lessons from life's maddening wonderfulness, the more we have to teach the young. The greater our age, the farther back our memory extends, making the elders our closest link to the ancestral wisdom of yesterday.

My godmother always told me that it takes twenty-five years of priesthood to really come into elderhood. By that time, an *olorisha* not only has accumulated priestly knowledge and insight, she has also become adept at integrating that knowledge into daily life—the true mark of a seasoned practitioner. Having accepted and worked their way into the role of a seer, the elders see their secular lives through a lens saturated with their spiritual awareness of Orisa and the teachings. This priest or priestess can then tap into this trove of personal experience to teach others. An elder who teaches younger initiates is known as a godparent.

Although true eldership takes time to acquire, technically a religious elder is anyone who has acquired more years of initiation than you have. Even if you are biologically older, in Orisa the more experienced practitioner remains your elder. Yoruba practitioners outside of the United States, such as in Nigeria, Brazil, and Cuba, understand that becoming qualified to teach others takes many years of training. In the United States, however, the standards entitling someone to function as a godparent have relaxed quite a bit. Here, priests of less than ten years duration are commonly found working as fully functioning elders for small and large communities of godchildren.

Such young priests can balance what they lack in years with a more advanced biological age, which should at least bring some life experience to their roles. When inexperienced priests are also young biologically, it can be quite dangerous for all concerned. Because experience is critical to understanding both life and Orisa, a priest young in both religious and biological age is often unprepared to guide others along a path they themselves are still relatively new to. These godparents may unwittingly create difficult situations and unhealthy relationships, which may cause their godchildren to suffer from their elders' premature leap into godparenthood. For this reason and others (which we'll go into shortly), it is essential to choose our elders carefully and wisely.

Whether you choose a godmother (*iya* in Yoruba, *madrina* in Spanish) or a godfather (*baba* in Yoruba, *padrino* in Spanish), your godparent should be a model of integrity, humility, patience, and clean heart. The elder should clearly demonstrate those qualities in the way he or she relates to you and others. You'll want a godparent who can point you toward the essence of the tradition and who embodies that essence in his or her daily life. Look for an elder who possesses ritual knowledge as well as spiritual insight, someone who values both internal and external processes and can support your learning in both.

Your godparent's role is to facilitate your spiritual growth by showing you how to work with Orisa and your *egun* to build your character, and heal and transform your life. They should provide you with the oracular teachings, guidance, and ritual alignments that will help reconnect you with your *ori* while deepening your relationship with the deities and your ancestors.

What you should *not* seek in an elder is someone who promises to save you or whom you expect to save you from any aspect of your life. Remember, although your godparent can instruct you in the teachings, you must take responsibility for how you use the teachings to better your life.

In order to adequately and effectively learn from your godparents, you must trust them. The safer and more comfortable you feel with your elder, the more willing and able you will be to share your most intimate thoughts, feelings, questions, and concerns—and the better able your godparent will be to respond to them. Safety is crucial, because it is the precursor to good communication. If anything has the power to make or break a relationship, it is how well and how fully two parties communicate. Your ability to talk with your elder about the hard issues that may arise between the two of you is especially important because at some point such problems will inevitably arise. As with any relationship, you'll run into difficulties that you will need to discuss and work together to resolve.

You should feel confident from the beginning that when you hit bumps on the road, both you and your elder will show up, roll up your sleeves, and work side by side to break through whatever barriers or challenges you encounter. You'll want to feel secure in the knowledge that the two of you will be able to look candidly and compassionately at one another and at yourselves. You must trust that you both can and will take responsibility for your respective part in any given situation, including mistakes that were made or important opportunities that were overlooked.

In the early years of your development, your godparent serves as an intermediary—your link to the teachings, ancestors, and deities. Ultimately, however, you and your godparent should work together toward building your personal connectedness with the Orisa. After all, these energies dwell all around and within you, and they are available to us all. The purpose of your learning is to eventually enable you to address the Orisa directly, to feel them within you, and to share your life with them on your own.

Look, Listen, and Learn

Before scholars began to record and document Yoruba teachings for broad dissemination, the tradition's ways were handed down orally from elder to *omo* (godchild). We now live in the age of books, CDs, and the Internet, new avenues for sharing information about Orisa. Nonetheless, elders today continue to teach their godchildren in much the same ways they always have: by doing and showing through example and repetition.

For instance, my godmother taught me how to give a *rogacion* (a cleansing to realign *ori*) by first allowing me to assist her as she gave *rogacions* to others. I was given simple tasks, such as prepping ingredients and arranging space for the cleansing. Although this was in a sense boring work, it was a wonderful opportunity. Every time my *madrina* said,

"No, that's too much water," or "Add a little more coconut to the plate," I learned something. And after I'd helped with all the preparations, I'd stand back a few feet and watch my *iya* while she worked. At one point she gave me a list detailing the *rogacion* procedure, so I could refer to it for later study, which I did. But I could never have learned from any piece of paper what I learned by simply observing. My schooling came through absorbing inflection and tone in her voice and taking in her subtle gestures, her precise movements, and the way she closed her prayers.

Many elders are like gushing springs, overflowing with knowledge and teaching. The best way to learn from them is to pay close attention to everything they do. Because their relationship with Orisa is thoroughly woven into their lives, they are likely to continually say and do things during the course of a day that are instructive, even while performing such mudane tasks as mopping the kitchen floor. If you're listening and watching closely, you'll catch these gems of wisdom as your elders offer them.

Western cultures place a high premium on a person's ability to answer questions and have a low tolerance for not knowing. Consequently, godchildren brought up in these regions frequently come to the tradition with piles of questions and a feverish desire to hunt down answers: *What is this for? Why do you do that? What does this mean? Where does that belong?*

Do not confuse your elders with God. Accept that you'll ask questions they cannot answer and hope they will be humble enough to say so honestly. This is as it should be, because, for all their access to oracles and divine energies, your godparents are living in the mystery of God just like you.

Of course, beyond those questions your elders can't answer are the many they won't answer. The old-school approach is refusing to respond to any questions whatsoever from the godchild, especially in the beginning stages of study. This may seem a bit brutal, and if the elder is abusive about it, it is. Apart from abuse, however, this approach comes from a place of deep understanding. The questions old-school elders answer are the ones you don't even realize you're asking. And as long as you're paying attention, these elders will teach you a great deal. Most will allow you to write down very little. Steeped in the wisdom of the oral tradition, traditional elders value the written word much less than they do direct experience. They remember how they learned by soaking up everything their elders did, said, intuited, and implied. Perhaps the most valuable lesson this approach instills in us is the need to utilize all our senses and to stay open to learning, regardless of the package it comes wrapped in.

When elders see a godchild's willingness to learn through quiet observation, most become more generous with their teachings. For the first few years I was with my godmother, I asked very few questions, except about very simple, basic things. After a while, she became more receptive. While we were in ritual settings, I became a fly on the wall and watched everything around me, especially the elders. I made myself as porous as possible to their conversations and the lessons interlacing them. Later on the drive home, I would ask my *madrina* questions, and she would answer freely most of the time.

Old-school elders don't stonewall us because they are sadists. By refusing to provide answers to our questions, they wisely choose to allow the answers to unfold for us over time. They prefer to wait for initiation and inner work to transform us into more seasoned spiritual vessels, fully capable of holding the insight and information we seek. Because our elders understand the stages of spiritual development, they know that some answers must wait until after we've passed through initiation and the life changes that prepare us to receive them.

With newer-school elders, it is all right to ask most kinds of questions. They'll even let you write stuff down and encourage you to access any and all resources, from people to books to online information. Most godparents today combine new- and old-school approaches. They value the oral traditions as well as more contemporary avenues of learning. They will answer some questions, while holding back on others. However, virtually all elders are likely to withhold answers to questions involving the details of ritual, since it is taboo to disclose this information to people who have not undergone the ceremonies.

Hierarchy and Power

An appreciation for hierarchy is woven into every aspect of Yoruba culture and religious life. In the Yoruba family I stayed with during my time in Nigeria, the children, aged nine to twenty-five, began each day by greeting their parents, their elders, and asking for their blessings. I was also taught to *dobale* (salute) before my elders first thing upon entering a room where there were other priests. At first glance, it might appear that the elders get all the perks, the first and best of everything. But in the Nigerian communities I was exposed to, I saw that hierarchy honored relationships where there was mutual respect. Although everyone had their roles, they seemed to attach little ego to their respective positions. People moved within the parameters given them, but in ways that did not violate the dignity of those lower than them in the hierarchy.

Unfortunately, among practitioners of Orisa tradition in the United States, hierarchy is often far less graceful. In many instances, it becomes a one-sided blessing, benefiting elders at the expense of younger initiates. Because the definition of what constitutes an elder has loosened considerably in the States, a priest who is essentially still a baby in terms of spiritual development can become a godparent, even though he may lack basic maturity, insight, and self-awareness. Godparents of this sort don't have far to go to become ego-driven maniacs, recklessly misusing their status and power, and leaving a trail of human wreckage in their wake. Senior priests who can legitimately claim elder status may also use their elderhood as an excuse for acting out and then refuse to take responsibility for the damage they incur while hiding behind their titles.

A built-in power imbalance always exists between an elder and a godchild; that is natural and appropriate. It makes sense to give wise and experienced teachers our respect and affection, to accept their decisions, and to receive their guidance with little or no challenge. But if not handled skillfully by both parties, this disparity can become a source of tremendous suffering for all involved.

Elders have tremendous influence on the lives of their godchildren. They face the delicate challenge of exerting their power without using it as a cover for their own weaknesses. They also must be willing to go one step further and to face those weaknesses humbly when their godchildren bring them to their attention, as they invariably will. At the very least, godparents must be willing to face the possibility that they may have weaknesses they are not aware of.

Abuse of power is an easy trap to fall into. We are all subject to the seductive pull of ego and image and our desire to seem important in the eyes of others. Sometimes abuse is relatively subtle: a slightly patronizing tone of voice or not saying hello to someone younger in initiation years. Other forms of abuse are more flagrant and treacherous, like using the oracle to forward your personal views, having sex with your godchildren or with clients who seek you out for spiritual guidance, or prescribing cleansings that aren't really necessary but will put extra money in your pocket. Even the most vigilant elder will regularly have occasion to stop, take an honest look, regroup, and try again. All godparents must commit themselves on a daily basis to staying flexible and humble, while simultaneously honoring their own wisdom and elder status.

Negotiating the intricacies of what is in many ways an adult/child relationship with an elder who is not your parent and may be chronologically younger than you can be difficult. I have found that there is an unspoken code in Orisa that equates respect for elders with silencing one's own truth. Godchildren should be respectful of their elders, yes, but respect should not be confused with hiding one's genuine opinions, beliefs, or feelings in order to please or accommodate an elder or to avoid confrontation.

I once talked to a woman who was planning to leave her *ile*, because her elder had hurt her feelings, and she couldn't find a way to tell him how she felt. I suggested she talk honestly with him, an option that, because of the way our hierarchies often work, had never occurred to her. She was lucky: her elder responded with integrity and apologized. The simple but significant act of telling and hearing the truth averted the dissolution of an important relationship.

In our efforts to honor the position of our godparents, we should never relinquish our responsibility to protect and honor our own voices. A godchild also should never be expected to meet one standard of ethical behavior and the godparent another. In the ideal situation, godparent and godchild build their relationship upon a foundation of openness, authenticity, and mutual respect, each knowing they will periodically need to surrender some control. As power struggles arise, they can then work together to address those issues openly, and with care.

Family Dynamics

When you commit yourself to a godparent, you are also entering a congregation, your *ocha* house or *ile.* This community will be your religious family, comprised of other godchildren at various stages of learning and initiation, with whom you will share godparent(s), fellowship, ritual, work, learning, and hopefully genuine affection.

People often come to a house looking for the warm and fuzzy aspects of family life. We want to be part of a group of like-minded souls who we hope will insulate us from loneliness and give us a sense of belonging. Creating that kind of environment with people who may be vastly different in most other areas of their lives but are drawn together because of a shared connection to the godparent of the house presents all sorts of challenges.

You should leave behind any romantic notions you have of what the religious family is and what it will give you. Most of us know from our families of origin that family can both help and hinder us, depending on how healthy the family and we are. Like all families, every *ocha* house has a unique blend of beauty and craziness, its own set of family dynamics.

According to family-systems theory, family members take on roles that define how they interact with one another and within groups outside the family. Family roles serve a dual purpose. They help people understand what's expected of them and feel more comfortable in meeting those expectations. In that way family roles help family systems to function. Dysfunction comes about when family roles limit people's ability to experience and express their individuality.

Without a doubt, many of the confining roles that play out in birth families get re-enacted in the *ile*. In my house, I was the good daughter, a role I was familiar with from my family of origin. As the favorite child, my job was never to rock the boat with my *madrina* and especially to avoid angering her. By doing so, I had a closer relationship with her than my godbrothers and sisters had. This had its advantages and, as I would discover many years into my relationship with her, its disadvantages. Among my *madrina*'s godchildren, there were other family roles being enacted: the outsider, the prince or princess, the caretaker, the underachiever, the scapegoat, and so on. The roles we all played in the house helped create a structure wherein everyone knew what to expect from each other in both positive and negative ways.

You can bet that you and the others in your religious house, including your godparents, will play out a whole slew of family roles that will be integral to the *ile*'s functioning. Most members of your house will be completely unaware that this is happening. This further strengthens the importance of being well connected to your inner self. When the roles people have taken on become too constricted, they will start to break free of them. I know from firsthand experience this can be extremely confusing and painful for everybody. The earlier you become aware of the roles you may be playing, the more conscious you are of family dynamics, the more empowered you will be to step beyond roles and to create authentic relationships with your elders.

Belonging to a house is a mixed bag. On one hand, much of an *ile*'s activities involve working together in ritual, which bonds people in profound ways. Connections formed in the *ile* can last a lifetime; your godbrothers and godsisters can indeed become family. But every negative thing that flows between siblings in our families of origin—power struggles, envy, competition, bullying—can also take place in the *ile,* particularly if the elders in charge are not paying close enough attention and are not leading the way and helping make family dynamics conscious.

If you join a house with the expectation of finding some sort of idealized substitute for your biological family, you may be surprised to find that the religious family can be just as dysfunctional as the biological one. If, however, you enter an *ocha* house knowing you will get what any family has to offer, you won't be too disappointed when the full and complex picture of your *ile* starts to show itself. Remember that although all families have their struggles, some are more dysfunctional than others, so take your time and choose your godparent and your spiritual house wisely.

Choosing an elder to guide you on the Yoruba path should be a gradual process, allowing ample time for elder and *omo* to get to know each other before committing. As a potential godchild, you are responsible for making an informed decision. Ask basic questions about what will be expected of you as an *omo*. Determine what your obligations will be to the Orisa who heads the house, to your elders and senior godchildren, and to the house itself. Look into what you are expected to contribute in terms of time and energy. Learn as much as you can about your potential godparent, who will likely become one of the most influential human beings in your adult life. Become familiar with the elder's approach to Orisa and the teachings. Make sure his or her orientation fits with the primary spiritual values that matter most to you. Do this investigative work before you step onto the path of initiation. Then, when you find the right person, commit yourself to learning from them.

---

1. My godmother, Obalade, taught me about the importance and nature of *ori*; much of this discussion comes from her teachings.

Chapter 9

The Path of Initiation

There is a saying among Orisa practitioners: Every head will find its house. Once you have found the elder you would like to be your godparent, he or she will ascertain via divination whether your official entry into the house is sanctioned by the ancestors and the gods and desired by your own head. If it is, you will begin the journey of initiation.

Remember that initiation is about a reclamation, not about reaching a destination. In life we never really arrive. We just continually accept (or reject) life's invitations to go deeper into alignment, joy, relationship, self-realization, and life purpose. Every time we think we've finally gotten "there," we discover that what we thought was a final stop is really only a pause. Moving into deeper alignment in one part of our lives frees us to notice some other area where *ori* wants us to make a change. When we decide we are willing to let Orisa guide our changes—on their terms, which won't always match ours—we're ready to make the commitment to initiation.

The initiation journey is divided into three main ritual stations: receiving *elekes*, receiving warriors, and entering the priesthood (making *ocha*). The pace of your passage along this ritual continuum is determined by your own readiness and the will of the gods, with the latter taking precedence. Each step of the way, the deities are consulted for their permission to proceed. Sometimes we may feel ready, but the Orisa tell us it's not the right time. The opposite may also happen: We may want to postpone taking the next step, but the gods want us to step forward into initiation now.

There is no formula for how long it takes to pass from one initiation to the next. For some people, the stages of *elekes,* warriors, and priesthood come quickly, perhaps in the space of a year or less; for others, it may take much longer. Regardless of the timing, each initiation marks an important stage in the life of a soul trying to reclaim its true path and purpose. Each initiation provokes a unique kind of movement in the initiate's life, a progression that moves you further along in the direction your head chose for you and deeper into relationship with the ancestors and the gods.

It would be a violation of my priesthood rites to disclose the particulars of the initiation rituals that I have undergone, so instead I'll talk about the principles underlying our rituals, but not the rituals themselves.

Elekes

Beads are to Yoruba culture what diamonds are to Western societies: a symbol of the highest beauty and prosperity, wellness, and good fortune.[2] The consecrated beaded necklaces worn by Yoruba initiates are called *elekes* (*ikeles* in Yoruba, *collares* in Spanish). Since these necklaces have been consecrated with ceremony and prayer, they are considered especially potent vessels of sacred endowment. Usually, *elekes* are given as a set of anywhere from two to six necklaces. Each *eleke* worn by an initiate bears the colors and patterns particular to one of the deities, and each is ritually amplified with a specific Orisa's *ashe.*

Thus, a novice who receives *elekes* is literally receiving the gods in bead form. *Elekes* tell of your affiliation with the tradition. They let others know that you have claimed this as your spiritual road and you have gained formal entry into the worldwide family of Orisa. Through the color, size, and pattern of their beads, *elekes* indicate the house or lineage to which you belong. *Elekes* tell others that you have made a formal commitment to learn and to grow in partnership with the Orisa, and that you have been "washed" into the tradition.

To the person wearing them, *elekes* serve as a reminder of the presence of Orisa and the breath of God—ever present, all surrounding, and indwelling. People often refer to the process of receiving *elekes* as a kind of baptism. This is a fitting term, because baptism brings renewal through water and prayer, two major elements of the *elekes* ritual. Like baptism, receiving *elekes* signifies the cleansing of a former existence and rebirth into a new life, one more conscious of divinity and God's work. In Yoruba tradition, the initial baptism of *elekes* brings together all of these elements for the purpose of realigning you with your *ori,* your personal divinity and keeper of your destiny.

Most of us who receive *elekes* remember this time as a crossroads in our lives, a moment when something about us began to change in a fundamental way. This life-defining change usually led to further changes by which our lives began to take on a more authentic shape. Looking back, many of us can now embrace what we were once unable to accept: Walking through that first door of initiation was a way of saying, *I am willing to be stripped of my former self, to leave behind something or someone.* In retrospect, we realize that things that had once worked no longer did and things that had once felt comfortable had become too tight. The old fabric that held our lives together began to unravel before our eyes, forcing us to re-examine old commitments that no longer made sense or served us. We probably felt compelled to put our lives under greater scrutiny, to look much more closely at how we were living.

One definition of baptism is "a painful new undertaking or experience."[3] Understanding this aspect of baptism helps us to make sense of the crossroads that *elekes* bring us to. The "new undertaking" is the attempt to literally extract a more authentic self from under the surface of our lives, to wake up and fully bring to life the person we came to Earth to be. The "new experience" is a life of love and deep relationship with the deities, who are here to support us in our awakening. The pain comes when we have to let go of people, habits, and circumstances that keep us closed to our truest selves and to Orisa.

Although receiving *elekes* is a gentler version of the stripping down that rebirths us during the priesthood rite, this initial reawakening is no less potent. To support us in adjusting to this realignment, one Orisa steps forward, determined through divination, to claim the novice. Because receiving *elekes* can unsettle and disorient us, this Orisa accompanies and assists us through our changes. (This guiding Orisa may or may not be the same one to claim your head for priesthood.)

Reciprocity

Because our tradition teaches that life is a circle of reciprocity, Olodumare expects us to give something back as a way of acknowledging what the Orisa and *elekes* give us. We reciprocate not in terms of payment and not out of fear or obligation, but to honor life's most basic rhythms and processes. We give in return because reciprocity is the law of nature: That which gives must be given to, and that which is given to must give. Becoming more conscious of life's cycles and our relationship to them is a key part of the Orisa tradition. What we give are our commitments, and there are several of them.

First and most fundamentally, we make a commitment to ourselves—to wake up, let go, and do whatever it takes so that *ori,* our head or soul, can unfold its work through us. Our second commitment is to the ancestors—our birth relatives, those of our religious lineage, and the blood lineage of our godparent. The ancestors are the ground upon which all of our healing, transformation, and realignment with *ori* take place. When we receive *elekes,* we commit to bringing *egun* to the forefront of our lives.

Our next commitment is to the deities, who work every day toward our healing and enlightenment. Then we have to be willing to follow their lead, to work with Orisa in conscious and active partnership as they support *ori* in fulfilling our chosen destiny. We also make a commitment to the head Orisa of our house, the deity who claims our godparent and who, through our elder, takes a primary role in guiding our process. We commit our time, energy, *ashe,* and love to nurturing the house and learning its traditions. We work to make sure the *ile* is solid, strong, and well cared for, as a demonstration of gratitude for the ways the house keeps us spiritually healthy and grounded.

Finally, receiving *elekes* means making a commitment to our *baba* or *iya* to take loving care of the spiritual seeds they plant in us. We honor this commitment by learning what our elders have to teach us, so that one day we too will have a spiritual storehouse from which to plant seeds in others. This is one of our core obligations as initiates: to do our part to ensure the continuation of Orisa tradition, preserving its values and teachings. Once the beauty of this tradition starts to work its healing power into our lives, we are obliged not to waste what has been given to us. In this manner, we honor the ancestors who carried these teachings through slavery, reassuring them that their hard work was not in vain.

The ceremony of *elekes* is like putting a match to dry kindling in a fireplace on a dark night. It strikes a spark that enables us to see things more clearly. It starts a flame of opportunity, allowing us to look at our lives through a different set of priorities centered in realignment with *ori* and in our relationship with the ancestors and Orisa. The *elekes* ritual provides the fuel for accelerating our process of re-centering and re-focusing our lives.

The Ten Commitments of Orisa Practitioners

Practice self-care.

Practice self-reflection.

Practice letting go.

Practice authenticity.

Practice seeing God within yourself.

Practice seeing God in others.

Practice humility.

Practice continual learning.

Practice choosing wisely.

Practice patience with yourself and others.

Warriors

Once a fire moves beyond the early stages, there usually comes a moment when it needs some stoking, tending, and feeding before it can burst into a full, lasting blaze. The ceremony of receiving warriors brings an infusion of energy to our process of continuing our re-attunement with *ori,* a strengthening and reinforcement of the spiritual fire that started when we received our beads.

The term *warriors* tells us that we are being given tools for some kind of battle and that these tools are intended to bring us victory. The battles that warriors help us win occur on many levels. The most rigorous and brutal fighting that most of us encounter on the journey back to an *ori*-aligned self, however, is that which occurs on our internal battle-fields. As anyone who has ever tried to live an authentic life knows, the most powerful enemy is always the one within. The person capable of hurting me most is usually me. The danger comes not from an outside enemy, but from our own decisions and indecisions, actions and inactions. The battles we most need help winning are not those brought upon us by others, but those waged by our own self-defeating, self-harming ways. Warriors are the allies, the weapons, and the soldiers that will help us win these battles. In so doing, the movement toward realignment, initiated by *elekes*, can continue steadily forward.

Claiming victory against the enemy within and remaining on the path of soul realignment requires the ability to call upon our warrior spirit. We have to draw out our internal resources for that struggle, while simultaneously internalizing the warrior qualities of four specific Orisa: Elegua, Ogun, Ochoosi, and Osun.

Through Elegua, gatekeeper and trickster, we learn to take greater responsibility for our choices and for how we undermine our own goodness. The ferocious but kind Ogun, master toolmaker who works non-stop in the bowels of Earth and within ourselves and gives us the strength to remain committed to self-reflection, provides us with the spiritual muscle to persevere on the road to our destiny as well as the courage to stay awake throughout our journey. Ochoosi, the supremely skilled hunter who never misses his mark, teaches us the benefits of a cool, clear, and focused head. He provides the calm diligence we will need to hunt down our internal foes. Osun, ever alert and at attention, serves as our internal warning system, letting us know when we are getting too far from our soul's agreements. Osun is the anchor that holds us to the pathways we are meant to follow.

The warriors bring us several vital lessons for authentic living on the path of Orisa. Lesson number one is that warriors do not turn their backs on each other. Warriors face the challenges of battle by working together, by supporting and covering each others' movements, just as we must learn to work in sync with Orisa and *ori* as they attempt to realign us. Warriors also must be willing to sacrifice their own comfort and safety for a greater cause, just as you too will be asked to exchange safety for healing, comfort for transformation, and image for authenticity.

The warriors give us tools for developing stamina and endurance on our spiritual journeys. From them we learn to reclaim the roads our heads have chosen for us and to cultivate a spiritual life rooted in humble character. They teach us that the blessings of this process come largely through struggle and that our journey requires tremendous staying power.

Our warriors teach us to have courage in the face of the necessary losses we will encounter when we begin to let

Orisa into the recesses of our lives. Warriors teach us bravery, so that when Orisa asks us, we are willing to face death for the sake of renewal and to kill what has become deadened within us so that something new can emerge.

Sometimes warriors are forced to survive on very little, like when Orisa strips away the familiar and easy, because those safe places are holding us back. At times the light illuminating the warriors' road grows dim, yet they must continue the struggle—such as when we are leaving behind an old self and cannot yet see the shape of who we are becoming. The warriors show us that although we may feel alone and afraid in the darkness, we must remain present and trust in the changes the Orisa are leading us through.

Often the process of reconnecting with *ori* and opening ourselves to Orisa requires a great deal of sacrifice, hard work, and spiritual bloodshed. When the battle heats up, as it inevitably will, a warrior feels the fear and does the work anyway. Passing through the initiation of receiving warriors ushers us into a higher level of spiritual challenge, insight, growth, and resources. Our warriors ask that we seek creative, mindful, and brave-hearted responses to the challenges that come with living an *ori*-centered, spirituality-based religious life. The beauty amid all this challenge is that as our work intensifies, our tool chest expands and our relationship with self and Orisa deepens.

My *madrina* taught me that realignment with *ori* could be a distressing and even traumatic experience. I learned that when someone has become used to walking tightened up and hunched over, it can be extremely stressful to be suddenly pulled upright. It's like spending your whole life being stiff and inflexible, unable to spread your legs more than twelve inches apart, then waking up one morning and being forced to do the splits.

When we're accustomed to walking out of step with ourselves, embarking upon a new road and responding to a different rhythm can feel overwhelming, even when the road and the rhythm are more in tune with what *ori* wants for us. Making this type of dramatic shift too quickly can do more damage than good. My godmother, for example, always refused to give a *rogacion* to people who were in the throes of sickness. She preferred waiting until they were well and therefore had the strength to receive the alignment. Most of us need to return to center gradually, because having adapted so well to living out of balance, a slower rebalancing feels safer and easier. Though walking through life off-kilter breaks us down over time, it often becomes second nature and can even become the focus that gives our lives purpose. Most of us need time to make the transition from crouching low to standing tall, from following somebody else's rhythm, which is easy to do, to dancing to our own, which requires a lot more from us.

So it is that in Orisa tradition each of us builds our spiritual fire in stages. Warriors help us acclimate to the growing heat and the rising flame of this fire, the purpose of which is to burn away the muck that distracts us from our true nature. The warrior phase of the journey is essential and a blessing, because once we arrive at the threshold of priesthood, the cleansing fire has reached its maximum strength. By then, our warriors have seasoned us a bit, and we have had some practice at letting go of what Orisa takes from us. In the process, we have hopefully become stronger and more connected to the deities, the ancestors, and ourselves—because we will need our full strength and complete trust in the gods for the next level of initiation. When we enter the inner sanctum and undergo the priesthood rites, the Orisa and *ori* pull us all the way up in one swift, decisive movement.

Priesthood

Initiation into the Orisa priesthood involves facing and moving beyond death. Initiation abruptly and in a sense violently severs us from our current existence. Usually this existence has become clogged with ways of thinking and living that undermine our ability to maintain oneness with God and to fully embrace our highest good. Entering the priesthood means sacrificing this too small life for one large enough to hold both our destiny and the Orisa's love.

"Making *ocha*" means walking away from our persona, the carefully constructed false self whose main concern is image. The ancestral elders who first divined these priesthood rituals recognized that image must be annihilated in order for transformation to take place. They knew that the gods can't do their work in us while we hide behind persona and that the Orisa don't care to know the you most people see.

When you cross the threshold into *igbodu* (the initiation room; literally, "sacred grove" in Yoruba), you leave at the door all the various roles you are accustomed to filling. It makes no difference whether you are smart, sexy, successful, or self-assured. It doesn't matter that you are someone's child, sibling, lover, boss, teacher, godchild, or friend. The Orisa do not care whether you are famous, rich, gorgeous, or powerful. All of this becomes extraneous and unimportant when we stand at the door to initiation.

What matters most to the elders is cutting away everything of your former life that is stale and hardened—whatever is unyielding to God and *ori*. What matters to the deities is that they see, feel, touch, and smell the real you. They want you fully exposed and denuded of all pretense, laid open and bare. Only then can the Orisa draw out and seat firmly the *ori* and destiny you brought to this life.

It is this realigned, pure, and unadulterated self that the elders ceremonially crown with the *ashe* of the Orisa who claims you. You become *iyawo* (literally, "wife of the gods" in Yoruba, but applicable to both men and women). Melded into spiritual and physical oneness with your head Orisa and reborn to a newly awakened consciousness, you are on your way to claiming your role as seer. At this point, you are fully opened to the deities, to seeing their presence alive and working in the world and within you. Most important, you are now spiritually aligned with yourself and with the sacred blueprint of your true purpose.

The purpose of making *ocha* is simply this:

- To pull you into a deeper, more meaningful relationship with God.
- To open the gateway to a more conscious connection with self by realigning you with your *ori*.
- To saturate your physical and energy bodies with the divine essence of the Orisa whose *ashe* will be most useful in helping you hold your alignment.

This level of initiation, like all the others, is not a resting place or a final destination along the path of Orisa. It is a crossroads, an opening. Being crowned with Orisa does not miraculously remedy all our pains. This gift, like the warriors, brings a new layer of challenges and tools.

Becoming an Orisa priest will not make you happy or make your life easy. But if you work diligently and allow the Orisa to do their work, the depth and integrity of your relationship with the deities and with yourself will create the opportunity for healing in your life. It will bring you increased joy, a profound beauty, and tremendous blessings.

---

2. John Mason (along with Henry Drewal) has written about the Yoruba and beads in a beautiful book called *Beads, Body, and Soul: Art and the Light in the Yoruba Universe*.

3. *The Concise Oxford Dictionary* (New York: Oxford University Press, 1990), 86.

Glossary

aborisha	Priest of Orisa, male or female
Aganyu	God of the volcano
aleyo	Someone who is uninitiated
ashe	Life-force energy, the essential nature of all things
baba	Father, godfather, *padrino*
babalawo	High priest of the Ifa priesthood order
babalorisha	Male priest of Orisa
bembe	Drum celebration in honor of the deities
Candomble	Afro-Brazilian version of Yoruba tradition
dobale	A salutation, greeting
ebo	An offering or cleansing
egun	Ancestor(s)
Elegua	God of the crossroads and choice
elekes	Consecrated beaded necklaces dedicated to the Orisa
elevation	A process of bringing peace to distressed spirits
house	Orisa *ile,* temple, or church
Ifa	A body of teachings; the Babalawo's oracle

igbodu	"Sacred grove"; the initiation room
Ikole Aye	The visible realm, Earth
Ikole Orun	The invisible real of gods and spirits
ile	Orisa temple, church, or house
imo	Knowledge
initiation	A process of spiritual rebirth
iya	Mother, godmother, *madrina*
iyalorisha	Female priest of Orisa
iyanifa	"Mother of Ifa"; high-ranking female initiate of Ifa
iyawo	A newly initiated priest, male or female
Lukumi	Non-catholicized version of Cuban Yoruba tradition
madrina	"Godmother" in Spanish; *iya*
misa	Ancestor ceremony
mojuba	Formal prayers
Obatala	God of white cloth, good character, and peace
ocha	Orisa tradition
odu	Scriptures of the Yoruba people
Ochoosi	God of the hunt
ogbon	Wisdom
Ogun	God of iron, courage, and truth; remover of obstacles

oju egun	"Face of the ancestors"; ancestral shrine
Olodumare	The Creator
olorisha	Priest or priestess of Orisa
Olorun	God, Source of all that is
omo	Child, godchild, student of Orisa
ona re'o	"May your road have blessing"; blessed road
ori	"Head"; one's essential self
ori'bi	"Bad head"; making poor choices in life by not using one's *ori* fully or wisely
ori're	"Good head"; using one's *ori* fully and wisely
ori inu	"Inner head"; the core of one's inborn nature
ori ode	"Outer head"; the physical container of the inner head
ori tutu	Cool headedness
Orisa	Yoruba divinities, messengers of Olodumare
Oshun	Goddess of fertility, healing, and the river
Osun	God who guards our spiritual balance
Oya	Goddess of winds; guardian of the cemetery
oye	Understanding
padrino	"Godfather" in Spanish; *baba*
rogacion	A cleansing to realign *ori*
Santeria	Cuban, catholicized version of Yoruba tradition

Shango	God of fire and lightening
vodun	Spirit or deity, in language of Fon peoples
warriors	Applies to several of the Orisa: Elegua, Ogun, Ochoosi, and Osun
Yemaya	Goddess of the sea, the full moon, and motherhood
Yoruba	The indiginous religion of the Yoruba people of southerwestern Nigeria

Bibliography

Abimbola, Wande. *Ifa: An Exposition of Ifa Literary Corpus.* Brooklyn, NY: Athelia Henrietta Press, 1997.

Abiodun, Rowland, Henry J. Drewal, and John Pemberton. *The Yoruba Artist.* Washington, DC: Smithsonian Institution Press, 1994.

Awolalu, J. O. *Yoruba Beliefs and Sacrificial Rites.* Brooklyn, NY: Athelia Henrietta Press, 1996.

Badejo, Diedre. *Osun Seegesi: The Elegant Deity of Wealth, Power, and Femininity.* Trenton, NJ: Africa World Press, 1995.

Barnes, Sandra (editor). *Africa's Ogun: Old World and New.* Bloomington, IN: Indiana University Press, 1989.

Bascom, William. *Ifa Divination: Communication Between Gods and Men in West Africa.* Bloomington, IN: Indiana University Press, 1991.

———. *Sixteen Cowries: Yoruba Divination from Africa to the New World.* Bloomington, IN: Indiana University Press, 1993.

Bramly, Serge. *Macumba: The Teachings of Maria-Jose, Mother of the Gods.* San Francisco: City Lights, 1994.

Brandon, George. *The Dead Sell Memories.* Bloomington, IN: Indiana University Press, 1997.

Canizares, Raul. *Cuban Santeria.* Rochester, VT: Inner Traditions, 1999.

————. *Walking with the Night.* Rochester, VT: Destiny Books, 1993.

Cortez, Julio Garcia. *The Osha: Secrets of the Yoruba-Santeria-Lucumi Religion in the United States and the Americas.* Brooklyn, NY: Athelia Henrietta Press, 2000.

Drewal, Henry J., and John Mason. *Beads, Body, and Soul: Art and Light in the Yoruba Universe.* Los Angeles: UCLA Fowler Museum of Cultural History, 1998.

Drewal, Henry J., and John Pemberton. *Yoruba: Nine Centuries of African Art and Thought.* New York: The Center for African Art, 1989.

Drewal, Margaret. *Gelede: Art and Female Power Among the Yorubas.* Bloomington, IN: Indiana University Press, 1992.

Epega, Afolabi, and Philip Neimark. *Sacred Ifa Oracle.* San Francisco: HarperSanFrancisco, 1995.

Fagg, William, and John Pemberton. *Yoruba: Sculpture of West Africa.* New York: Knopf, 1982.

Falade, Fasina. *Ifa: The Keys to Its Understanding.* Lynwood, CA: Ara Ifa Publishing, 1999.

————. *Ijo Orunmila.* Lynwood, CA: Ara Ifa Publishing, 1998.

Fama, Chief. *Fundamentals of the Yoruba Religion (Orisa Worship).* San Bernardino, CA: Ile Orunmila Publications, 1993.

Fatunmbi, Fa'lokun. *Awo, Ifa, and the Theology of Divination.* New York: Original Publications, 1992.

————. *Iba'se Orisa, Ifa Proverbs, Folktales, Sacred History and Prayer.* New York: Original Publications, 1994.

————. *Iwa Pele: The Search for the Source of Santeria and Lucumi.* New York: Original Publications, 1991.

———. Several pamphlets about the main Yoruba divinities. New York: Original Publications, 1992–1996.

Galembo, Phyllis. *Divine Inspiration.* Albuquerque: University of New Mexico Press, 1993.

Gonzalez-Wippler, Migene. *Santeria the Religion: Faith, Rites, Magic.* St. Paul, MN: Llewellyn Publications, 1996. (This author also has written five other books on this topic.)

Idowu, E. Bolaji. *Olodumare: God in Yoruba Belief.* New York: Original Publications, 1995.

Karode, Baba Ifa. *Handbook of Yoruba Religion.* York Beach, ME: Samuel Wieser, 1994.

———. *Ojise: Messenger of the Yoruba Tradition.* York Beach, ME: Samuel Wieser, 1996.

Landes, Ruth. *City of Women.* Albuquerque, NM: University of New Mexico Press, 1994.

Lele, Ochani. *The Secrets of Afro-Cuban Divination.* Rochester, VT: Destiny Books, 2000.

Lindsay, Arturo (editor). *Santeria Aesthetics in Contemporary Latin American Art.* Washington, DC: Smithsonian Institution Press, 1996.

Lucas, J. Olumide. *The Religion of the Yorubas.* Brooklyn, NY: Athelia Henrietta Press, 1996.

Mason, John. *Black Gods: Orisa Studies in the New World.* Brooklyn, NY: The Yoruba Theological Archministry, 1985.

———. *Four New World Yoruba Rituals.* Brooklyn, NY: The Yoruba Theological Archministry, 1993.

———. *Olookun: Owner of Rivers and Seas.* Brooklyn, NY: The Yoruba Theological Archministry, 1996.

————. *Orin Orisa: Songs of the Orisa*. Brooklyn, NY: The Yoruba Theological Archministry, 1992.

Murphy, Joseph. *Santeria: An African Religion in America*. Boston: Beacon Press, 1988.

Neimark, Philip. *Way of the Orisa*. San Francisco: HarperSanFrancisco, 1993.

Ogunyemi, Yemi D. *Introduction to Yoruba Philosophy, Religion, and Literature*. Brooklyn, NY: Athelia Henrietta Press, 1998.

————. *The Covenant of the Earth: Yoruba Religious and Philosophical Narratives*. Brooklyn, NY: Athelia Henrietta Press, 1998.

Peel, J. D. Y. *Religious Encounter and the Making of the Yoruba*. Bloomington, IN: Indiana University Press, 2001.

Thompson, Robert Farris. *Flash of the Spirit*. New York: Random House, 1983.

————. *Face of the Gods: Art and Altars of Africa and the African Americas*. New York: The Museum for African Art, 1993.

Velez, Maria Teresa. *Drumming for the Gods: The Life and Times of Felipe Garcia Villamil, Santero, Palero, and Abakua*. Philadelphia: Temple University Press, 2000.

Index